The Entrepreneurial Mindset Paradigm

Kay Kay Singh

Copyright ©2024 Kay Kay Singh

All rights reserved. No part of this book may be reproduced, distributed, or transmitted in any form or by any means, including photocopying, recording, or other electronic or mechanical methods, without the prior written permission of the publisher, except in the case of brief quotations used in critical reviews and certain other noncommercial purposes permitted by copyright law.

About the Author's

Kay Kay Singh started his entrepreneurial journey back in 1989 in India and now is a highly accomplished entrepreneur and real estate investor with a diverse background and impressive track record. As the Founder & CEO of Grow Rich Capital and President of Hoosier Group of Companies, Singh has built a multifaceted business empire spanning from gas stations, laundromats, an event center, single and multifamily real estate investments.

Singh's journey in the United States began as a Microsoft Certified System Engineer before he transitioned into entrepreneurship in 2001. Over the past three and half decades, he has successfully owned and operated multiple diverse businesses.

Singh's expertise extends beyond just owning businesses. Singh has been a multifamily and a mindset coach for 4 years. He has become a respected voice in the entrepreneurial and multifamily investment communities, frequently appearing as a guest speaker on various podcasts and panels to share his insights and experiences.

With his extensive background in multiple industries and his proven ability to adapt and thrive in different business environments, Kay Kay Singh brings a wealth of practical knowledge and real-world experience to "The Entrepreneurial Mindset Paradigm." His journey from a tech professional to a successful multi-business owner exemplifies the power of entrepreneurial thinking and strategic risk-taking, making him well-qualified to guide readers on their own paths to success.

Dedicated To

This book is dedicated to my late beloved parents. Your unwavering love, wisdom, and guidance laid the foundation for the principles shared in these pages. Father, your dedication to justice as an advocate and mother's boundless compassion taught me that true success stems from integrity and perseverance. Though you are no longer here to witness this achievement, your legacy lives on through every chapter.

Quick Start Guide: Your 90-Day Entrepreneurial Transformation

Welcome to your entrepreneurial journey! While I recommend reading this book cover-to-cover, I understand you might be eager to start implementing right away. This guide provides a comprehensive 90-day action plan to begin transforming your entrepreneurial mindset and practices immediately.

Month 1: Foundation Building
Week 1-2: Mindset Reset & Vision
Days 1-7: Mindset Development
- Take the Entrepreneurial Mindset Assessment (Chapter 1)
- Start a daily "Win Journal" - write down three achievements each day
- Identify and write down your five most limiting beliefs
- Spend one day on each belief, reframing it into an empowering statement
- Begin 15-minute daily meditation practice

Days 8-14: Vision Creation
- Write your "Big Why" - what drives you as an entrepreneur?
- Create a detailed 3-year vision for your business
- Break your vision into annual goals
- Further divide into quarterly objectives
- Share your vision with two trusted accountability partners
- Create a vision board for visual motivation

Week 3-4: Personal Systems
Days 15-21: Time Mastery
- Implement the Pomodoro Technique (25 minutes work, 5 minutes break)
- Create time blocks for your five most important daily tasks
- Conduct a full week time audit
- Identify and eliminate your top three time wasters
- Design your ideal week schedule
- Test and refine your daily routine

Days 22-30: Building Resilience
- Increase meditation to 20 minutes daily
- Create your "Failure Resume" - list past setbacks and lessons learned
- Develop your personal resilience ritual for handling setbacks
- Establish a morning success routine
- Create an evening reflection practice
- Build your stress management toolkit

Month 2: Business Development
Week 5-6: Network & Relationships
Days 31-45: Strategic Connection Building
- Reach out to five new potential connections each week
- Join two relevant professional groups or online communities
- Schedule three coffee meetings with potential mentors
- Create your networking strategy document
- Develop your personal brand statement
- Start a relationship management system
- Begin weekly networking review and planning

Week 7-8: Innovation & Systems
Days 46-60: Business Enhancement
- Conduct a full business systems audit
- Identify three processes to automate
- Test two new business ideas
- Create standard operating procedures for core processes
- Implement one new technology solution
- Develop your innovation pipeline
- Establish weekly innovation brainstorming sessions

Month 3: Integration & Scale
Week 9-10: Leadership & Team
Days 61-75: Leadership Development
- Take the Leadership Assessment (Chapter 12)
- Create or refine your delegation system
- Have in-depth conversations with each team member
- Document your leadership philosophy
- Establish team communication protocols
- Create your team development plan
- Set up regular team feedback sessions

Week 11-12: Financial Mastery & Future Planning
Days 76-90: Financial Intelligence & Integration
- Take the Financial Intelligence Assessment (Chapter 15)
- Create a comprehensive financial dashboard
- Set up daily, weekly, and monthly financial review habits
- Develop your cash flow forecasting system
- Create your profit optimization plan
- Design your quarterly business review process
- Build your annual planning system

Daily Non-Negotiables
Complete these every day:
1. Read one chapter of this book
2. Take two specific actions toward your goals
3. Document your progress and insights
4. Practice intentional self-care
5. Review your vision and goals

Weekly Check-In Questions
Review every Sunday:
1. What were my top three wins this week?
2. What challenges did I face and how did I handle them?
3. What key lessons did I learn?
4. What adjustments do I need to make next week?
5. How am I progressing toward my quarterly goals?
6. Am I maintaining work-life balance?

Monthly Review Process
Conduct on the last day of each month:
1. Review all weekly check-ins
2. Measure progress against quarterly goals
3. Adjust next month's priorities as needed
4. Celebrate wins and analyze setbacks
5. Update your action plan for the next 30 days

Remember
- Focus on progress, not perfection
- Small consistent actions create lasting change
- Modify this plan to fit your specific needs
- Keep revisiting the book for deeper insights
- Trust the process and stay committed

Your First Action Step
Start right now by taking the Entrepreneurial Mindset Assessment and scheduling your daily reading time for the next 90 days.

Emergency Response Plan
When facing challenges:
1. Breathe and step back
2. Review your "Big Why"
3. Consult relevant book chapters
4. Reach out to your support network
5. Focus on the next small step forward
6. Use your resilience ritual
7. Schedule a mentor check-in

This Quick Start Guide is your roadmap to meaningful transformation. While it doesn't replace the deep insights and strategies in the full book, it gives you a structured way to implement key concepts systematically over 90 days.

Your entrepreneurial transformation begins today. Take your first step now.

Table of Contents

Preface 1

Introduction 3

Chapter 1: The Entrepreneurial Mindset - Rewiring Your Brain for Success 11

Chapter 2: Embracing Failure - Your Steppingstone to Success 21

Chapter 3: The Vision Quest - Crafting Your Entrepreneurial Dream 31

Chapter 4: Building Resilience - Your Entrepreneurial Armor .. 41

Chapter 5: The Growth Mindset Revolution - Unleashing Your Potential 51

Chapter 6: Time Mastery - Harnessing Your Most Valuable Resource 61

Chapter 7: The Network Effect - Building Relationships That Matter 71

Chapter 8: Financial Intelligence - The Language of Business Success 81

Chapter 9: Innovation Ignition - Sparking Creativity in Your Venture 91

Chapter 10: The Confidence Equation - Building Unshakeable Self-Belief 101

Chapter 11: Decision Mastery - Forging Your Entrepreneurial Destiny 111

Chapter 12: The Leadership Leap - Inspiring Others to Achieve Greatness 121

Chapter 13: Focus Fundamentals - Cutting Through the Noise.. 131

Chapter 14: The Balance Beam - Thriving in Work and Life.. 143

Chapter 15: Adaptability - Your Competitive Edge in a Changing World............ 153

Chapter 16: The Delegation Revelation - Unleashing Your Team's Potential 163

Chapter 17: Emotional Intelligence - Your Secret Weapon in Business 173

Chapter 18: The Persistence Principle - Never Give Up, Never Surrender 187

Chapter 19: The Ethics Advantage - Building a Business with Integrity............ 199

Chapter 20: Your Entrepreneurial Odyssey - Putting It All Together............ 209

Preface

Welcome to "The Entrepreneurial Mindset Paradigm: Rewiring Your Brain for Business Success," a journey into the heart of what makes entrepreneurs tick. This book isn't just about business strategies or market analysis—it's about the mindset that drives innovation, resilience, and success in the ever-changing world of entrepreneurship.

As an entrepreneur myself, I've experienced firsthand the rollercoaster of starting and growing businesses. I've tasted the thrill of success and the bitter sting of failure. But through it all, I've come to realize that the true determinant of entrepreneurial success isn't just about having the right idea or the most resources. It's about cultivating the right mindset.

In these pages, we'll together explore the core principles that set successful entrepreneurs apart. From embracing failure as a steppingstone to success, to harnessing the power of persistence, to building unshakeable confidence, we'll delve deep into the psychological and emotional aspects of entrepreneurship.

This book is the culmination of years of personal experience, extensive research, and insights gleaned from some of the world's most successful entrepreneurs. It's designed to be more than just a read—it's a toolkit for transformation. Each chapter concludes with practical exercises, key takeaways and action steps to help you apply these principles in your own entrepreneurial journey as you read this book. Follow the steps in each chapter and do the exercise as you read and do it again and again.

Whether you're a seasoned business owner looking to level up, an aspiring entrepreneur with a world-changing idea, or simply someone seeking to cultivate a more proactive and innovative approach to life, this book has something for everyone at any stage of the entrepreneurial journey.

Remember, entrepreneurship isn't just about what you do—it's about who you become in the process. It's about pushing past your comfort zone, embracing challenges as opportunities for growth, and consistently showing up for yourself and your dreams. Entrepreneurship is a marathon not a sprint.

As you embark on this journey, I encourage you to approach each chapter with an open mind and a willingness to challenge your assumptions. The path of an entrepreneur is not for the faint of heart, but for those who dare to dream big and work tirelessly and step outside their comfort zone to turn those dreams into reality.

So, are you ready to revolutionize your mindset and unleash your full entrepreneurial potential? Let's begin this transformative journey together.

Your fellow entrepreneur and guide,

Kay Kay Singh

Introduction

> The biggest risk is not taking any risk. In a world that's changing quickly, the only strategy that is guaranteed to fail is not taking risks."
> - Mark Zuckerberg

Picture this: It's 2000, and a young woman named Sara Blakely is getting ready for a party. As she puts on her cream-colored pants, she grimaces at her reflection. The panty lines are visible, and the fit isn't flattering. In that moment of frustration, most people would simply change clothes or accept defeat. But Sara? She saw an opportunity.

Fast forward to today, and Sara Blakely is the founder of Spanx, a billion-dollar company that revolutionized the shapewear industry. But here's the kicker: Sara had no background in fashion, no business degree, and no startup capital. What she did have was an entrepreneurial mindset—a way of thinking that turned a simple clothing frustration into a global empire.

Now, you might be thinking, "That's great for Sara, but I'm not trying to invent the next big thing in underwear." Fair enough. But here's the truth bomb I'm about to drop on you: The entrepreneurial mindset isn't just for people starting businesses. It's a superpower that can transform every aspect of your life, whether you're launching a startup, climbing the corporate ladder, or just trying to navigate the wild rollercoaster we call life.

The Science of Success: It's All in Your Head (Literally)

You've probably heard the phrase "mindset is everything." Well, it turns out that's not just some motivational poster. It's science, baby.

Dr. Carol Dweck, a Stanford psychologist and all-around badass in the field of human motivation, spent decades researching what separates high achievers from everyone else. Her groundbreaking work revealed that success isn't just about talent or intelligence—it's about mindset.

Dweck identified two primary mindsets: fixed and growth. People with a fixed mindset believe their abilities are set in stone. They're the ones who say things like, "I'm just not good at math" or "I'm not a creative person." On the flip side, those with a growth mindset believe they can develop their abilities through effort and learning. They're the ones who say, "I haven't figured it out... yet."

Here's where it gets really interesting: Dweck's research showed that entrepreneurs with a growth mindset were more likely to:

- Persist in the face of setbacks
- Seek out challenges and new opportunities
- Learn from criticism and feedback
- Achieve higher levels of success over time

In other words, the entrepreneurial mindset isn't just some feel-good concept—it's a scientifically validated approach to success.

The Entrepreneurial Mindset: Your Secret Weapon

So, what exactly is this entrepreneurial mindset? It's a way of thinking and acting that embraces:

1. Opportunity Recognition: Seeing possibilities where others see pipeline ends.

2. Risk-Taking: Not reckless gambling, but calculated risks based on informed decisions.
3. Innovation: Constantly seeking new and better ways to do things.
4. Resilience: Bouncing back from failures and setbacks stronger than before.
5. Adaptability: Thriving in uncertainty and rapidly changing environments.
6. Growth-Oriented Thinking: Believing in the power of continuous learning and improvement.

Now, I know what some of you are thinking: "But Kay Kay, I'm not a 'natural entrepreneur.' I don't have that special X-factor." Well, I've got news for you: That's bullshit. (Sorry, not sorry for the language. We're keeping it real here.)

The truth is the entrepreneurial mindset isn't something you're born with—it's something you develop. It's a set of mental habits, discipline and attitudes that you can cultivate and strengthen over time. And that's exactly what this book is going to help you do.

Your Roadmap to Success

Over the next chapters, we're going to dive deep into each aspect of the entrepreneurial mindset. You'll learn:

- How to rewire your brain for success (yes, it's possible)
- Strategies for turning failures into steppingstones (because let's face it, you're going to fail... a lot)
- Techniques for spotting opportunities that others miss (it's like having entrepreneurial superpowers)
- Methods for building unshakeable confidence (even when you feel like a total impostor)
- Ways to cultivate resilience and grit (because success is a marathon, not a sprint)
- But here's the deal: This isn't just another self-help book filled with fluffy ideas and generic advice. We're going to get our hands dirty. Each chapter includes:

- Real-world case studies of entrepreneurs who've been in the trenches
- Practical exercises to help you apply the concepts immediately
- Action steps to keep you moving forward
- Brutally honest reality checks (because sometimes you need a kick in the pants)

The Hard Truth: This isn't Easy Task, otherwise everyone would have been an entrepreneur.

Let's be real for a second. Developing an entrepreneurial mindset isn't all sunshine and rainbows. It's going to challenge you. It's going to make you uncomfortable. There will be moments when you want to chuck this book across the room and go back to your comfort zone.

But here's the thing: Discomfort is where the magic happens. It's in those moments of doubt, fear, and uncertainty that you have the opportunity to grow the most. As Brené Brown, researcher and vulnerability expert, puts it: "Vulnerability is the birthplace of innovation, creativity, and change."

Throughout this book, I'm going to share some of my own struggles and failures. Not because I like airing my dirty laundry, but because I want you to know that everyone—yes, even successful entrepreneurs—deals with limited beliefs, self-doubt and setbacks. The difference is in how we respond to those challenges.

Your Journey Starts Now

Are you ready to transform your mindset and unlock your entrepreneurial potential? Are you willing to challenge your assumptions, push past your comfort zone, and become the badass, opportunity-seizing dynamo you were meant to be?

If you're nodding your head (or even if you're hesitating but feeling a little spark of curiosity), then let's do this thing. Nothing happens if you do not get excited.

Turn the page, and let's start rewiring your brain for success. Your entrepreneurial journey begins now.

Action Step: Before you dive into Chapter 1, take a moment to complete the Entrepreneurial Mindset Assessment on the next page. This will give you a baseline to track your progress as you work through the book. Be honest with yourself—remember, we're all starting somewhere, and the only person you're competing with is yourself.

Let's get after it.

HOW TO USE THIS BOOK

This isn't a passive read. It's an interactive experience designed to challenge your assumptions, expand your thinking, and push you out of your comfort zone. Here's how to get the most out of it:

1. Take the Assessments: Each chapter includes self-assessment tools to help you gauge where you stand on various aspects of the entrepreneurial mindset.
2. Do the Exercises: Don't skip the activities and reflection questions. They're designed to deepen your understanding and personalize the concepts.
3. Share Your Journey: Consider reading this with a group of fellow entrepreneurs or a mentor. The discussions and shared insights will enrich your experience.
4. Revisit and Reflect: Entrepreneurial growth is ongoing. Plan to revisit this book periodically as you progress in your journey and take the assessment before and after reading each time.

Are You Ready to Transform Your Mindset?

The path of an entrepreneur is not for the faint of heart. It will test you, challenge you, and push you to your limits. But with the right mindset, it can also be the most rewarding journey of your life.

As we embark on this exploration together, I invite you to approach each page with an open mind and a willingness to change. The insights and strategies in this book have the power to revolutionize not just your business, but your entire approach to life.

Before we dive into the first chapter, let's establish your starting point. Take the Entrepreneurial Mindset Assessment. This will help you identify your current strengths and areas for growth as we begin this transformative journey together.

Remember, the most successful entrepreneurs aren't necessarily the smartest or the most talented. They're the ones who cultivate the right mindset—a mindset of growth, resilience, and unwavering determination.

Here's an Entrepreneurial Mindset Assessment worksheet and Take the Following Assessment:

ENTREPRENEURIAL MINDSET ASSESSMENT:

Introduction

Rate yourself on a scale of 1-5 for each statement below:

    1 = Strongly Disagree
    2 = Disagree
    3 = Neutral
    4 = Agree
    5 = Strongly Agree

1. I see failures as learning opportunities rather than personal defects. Rating: ____

2. I actively seek out challenges that push me out of my comfort zone. Rating: ____

3. I'm comfortable taking calculated risks in pursuit of my goals. Rating: ____

4. When faced with obstacles, I persist and find alternative solutions. Rating: ____

5. I regularly set ambitious goals for myself and work diligently to achieve them. Rating: ____

6. I'm open to feedback and criticism, seeing them as chances to improve. Rating: ____

7. I believe my skills and abilities can be developed through effort and learning. Rating: ____

8. I'm quick to adapt my strategies when circumstances change. Rating: ____

9. I actively look for opportunities where others see problems. Rating: ____

10. I take full responsibility for my successes and failures. Rating: ____

11. I regularly step out of my comfort zone to learn new skills. Rating: ____

12. I'm comfortable with uncertainty and ambiguity in business situations. Rating: ___

13. I network actively and build relationships with diverse groups of people. Rating: ___

14. I consistently follow through on my commitments, even when it's difficult. Rating: ___

15. I'm able to maintain a positive outlook, even in challenging situations. Rating: ___

Scoring:
Add up your total score: ___

60-75: Strong Entrepreneurial Mindset
45-59: Developing Entrepreneurial Mindset
30-44: Emerging Entrepreneurial Mindset
15-29: Beginning Entrepreneurial Mindset

Reflection:

1. Which areas did you score highest in?

2. Which areas do you feel need the most improvement?

3. What specific actions can you take to strengthen your entrepreneurial mindset?

Remember, this assessment is a starting point. As you work through the book, you'll develop strategies to improve in all these areas. Revisit this assessment periodically to track your progress and identify areas for continued growth.

Chapter 1

The Entrepreneurial Mindset - Rewiring Your Brain for Success

---
The mind is everything.
What you think you become."
– Buddha

In this chapter I will show you how to fundamentally transform your entrepreneurial journey by mastering the most powerful tool at your disposal - your mindset. Through cutting-edge neuroscience and real-world examples, learn how successful entrepreneurs leverage both growth mindset and emotional intelligence to turn challenges into opportunities.

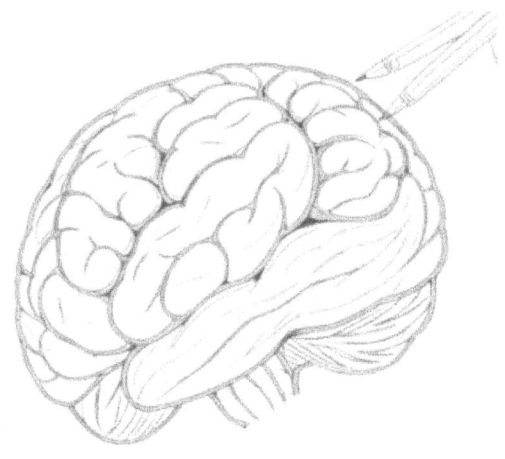

As the sun rises over Palo Alto, Elon Musk stands in the SpaceX factory, his eyes fixed on the remnants of the third failed Falcon 1 rocket launch. It's 2008, and both SpaceX and Tesla are teetering on the brink of bankruptcy. For most, this would be the end of the road. But Musk isn't like most people. His mind is already racing, analyzing the failure and planning the next launch. This moment, seemingly one of defeat, would later be recognized as a turning point, not just for Musk's companies, but for the entire space industry. What made the difference? It wasn't just Musk's technical knowledge or financial resources. It was his mindset - an unwavering belief that he could solve any problem, overcome any obstacle, and ultimately succeed where others had failed. This, fellow entrepreneurs, is the power of the entrepreneurial mindset - a force that can transform setbacks into steppingstones and challenges into opportunities for growth

What made the difference? It wasn't just Musk's technical knowledge or his financial resources. It was his mindset - an unwavering belief that he could solve any problem, overcome any obstacle, and ultimately succeed where others had failed.

This, my fellow entrepreneurs, is the power of the entrepreneurial mindset. It's not just about positive thinking or blind optimism. It's about rewiring your brain to see opportunities where others see obstacles, to learn from failures instead of being defeated by them, and to persist in the face of seemingly unconquerable challenges.

The Science of Mindset: It's All in Your Head

But don't just take my word for it. Let's look at what science has to say about the power of mindset.

Dr. Carol Dweck, a renowned psychologist at Stanford University, has spent decades researching the impact of mindset on success. Her groundbreaking work has identified two primary mindsets: fixed and growth.

Those with a fixed mindset believe their abilities and intelligence are static - they're either born with certain talents or they're not. They often say things like "I'm just not good with numbers" or "I wasn't born to be a leader." This mindset becomes a self-fulfilling prophecy, limiting their potential and causing them to avoid challenges for fear of failure. They see effort as fruitless and feedback as personal criticism. In contrast, those with a growth mindset believe their abilities can be developed through dedication and hard work. They view challenges as opportunities to learn, embrace effort as the path to mastery, and see feedback as valuable information for improvement. When faced with setbacks, they don't question their intelligence or abilities; instead, they think "I haven't figured this out...yet." This powerful three-letter word - "yet" - encapsulates the entire growth mindset philosophy. They understand that even geniuses like Einstein had to work hard to develop their capabilities, and that the brain is like a muscle that grows stronger with exercise and consistent practice.

In one study, Dweck and her colleagues followed hundreds of students transitioning to junior high school, a challenging time for many. They found that students with a growth mindset - those who believed their intelligence could be developed - outperformed those with a fixed mindset, even when they entered with equal academic achievement.

Growth vs Fixed Mindset

Growth Mindset	Fixed Mindset
"Failures are opportunities to learn"	"Failures define my abilities"
"Effort leads to mastery"	"Talent is natural or nothing"
"Challenges help me grow"	"Challenges expose weaknesses"
"Feedback is constructive"	"Feedback is criticism"
"I can learn anything"	"My abilities are fixed"
"Success comes from growth"	"Success proves my worth"

But here's where it gets really interesting for us entrepreneurs: this same principle applies in business. A study published in the Journal of Entrepreneurship found that entrepreneurs with a growth mindset were more likely to persevere in the face of challenges, seek out learning opportunities, and ultimately achieve greater success in their ventures. These growth-minded entrepreneurs approached problems differently - instead of seeing a failing product as a personal failure, they saw it as data. Instead of viewing a lost client as proof of their inadequacy, they asked themselves "What can I learn from this?" When faced with tough competition, rather than giving up, they doubled down on innovation and improvement. The study found that entrepreneurs with a growth mindset were 45% more likely to pursue additional ventures after a setback, 65% more likely to seek help, mentorship and feedback, and showed 73% higher resilience scores compared to their fixed-mindset peers.

Think about Sara Blakely, the founder of Spanx, who spent seven years selling fax machines door-to-door while developing her product. She didn't let rejection or lack of experience in the fashion industry stop her. Instead, she saw each "no" as an opportunity to refine her pitch, each setback as a chance to improve her product. This growth mindset approach ultimately led her to become the youngest self-made female billionaire in history. The message is clear: in entrepreneurship, it's not your initial talents that determine your success - it's your mindset and willingness to grow, learn, and adapt.

The Neuroscience of Belief: Where Brain Science Meets Business Success

Now, let's dive a little deeper into the brain. Neuroscientists have discovered that our beliefs literally shape our reality. When we believe we can achieve something, our reticular activating system (RAS) - a bundle of nerves at our brainstem - starts filtering for information that supports that belief.

Think about it like this: have you ever decided to buy a certain car, and suddenly you start seeing that car everywhere? That's your RAS at work, filtering information based on what you've deemed important.

As entrepreneurs, when we cultivate a mindset of possibility and growth, our brains start noticing opportunities and solutions we might have otherwise missed. It's not magic - it's neuroscience.

From Fixed to Growth: The Entrepreneurial Paradigm Shift

So, how do we shift from a fixed to a growth mindset? Let's break it down:

1. Embrace Challenges: Challenging situations provide invaluable opportunities for personal and professional growth. By actively seeking out these challenges, you can push the boundaries of your abilities and develop new skills that propel you forward. This mindset of embracing obstacles, rather than avoiding them, fosters a sense of curiosity and a willingness to learn, which are essential traits of successful entrepreneurs.

2. Persist in the Face of Setbacks: In entrepreneurship, failure is an inevitable part of the journey. However, a growth mindset allows you to reframe these setbacks as valuable learning experiences, rather than personal shortcomings. When faced with a roadblock, a growth-oriented entrepreneur will reflect on the situation, analyze what went wrong, and strategize ways to overcome the challenge. This persistence and dedication to continuous improvement are hallmarks of the entrepreneurial spirit.

3. See Effort as the Path to Mastery: Developing expertise and mastering new skills requires consistent, dedicated effort. Entrepreneurs with a growth mindset understand that hard work is not just a means to an end, but rather the very process by which they hone their abilities and achieve their goals. They approach challenges with a sense

of determination and a willingness to put in the necessary time and energy to overcome obstacles and reach new levels of excellence.

4. Learn from Criticism: Feedback, whether positive or negative, is a valuable tool for personal and professional growth. Individuals with a fixed mindset often take criticism personally and become defensive, while those with a growth mindset view it as an opportunity to identify areas for improvement. By approaching feedback with an open and receptive attitude, entrepreneurs can gain invaluable insights that inform their decision-making and guide their future actions.

5. Find Lessons and Inspiration in Others' Success: It can be easy to feel threatened or discouraged by the achievements of others, but a growth mindset allows entrepreneurs to reframe these situations. Instead of seeing others' success as a source of competition, entrepreneurs with a growth mindset use it as inspiration and leverage it as a learning opportunity. They seek to understand the strategies, habits, and mindsets that contributed to their peers' accomplishments, and then apply those lessons to their own entrepreneurial journey.

The Unexpected Connection: Mindset and Innovation

Now, here's something that might surprise you: the entrepreneurial mindset isn't just crucial for business success - it's a key driver of innovation across various fields.

Take the world of sports, for instance. In 1954, it was widely believed that running a four-minute mile was physically impossible. The four-minute barrier had stood for so long that it had become more than just a physical challenge - it was a psychological wall that seemed insurmountable. Leading medical experts and physiologists of the time warned that the human body would break down under the strain, with some even suggesting that the heart would explode from the effort. But Roger Bannister, a medical student at the time, approached the challenge differently. He combined his scientific knowledge with relentless training, innovative methods, and most importantly, an unshakeable belief that the impossible was possible. On a cold, wet day on May 6, 1954, Bannister did what experts said couldn't be done - he ran a mile in 3 minutes and 59.4 seconds, shattering not just the record, but the mental barriers that had held back athletes for generations.

Here's the kicker: within just 46 days, Australian runner John Landy also broke the four-minute barrier. Within three years, 16 other runners had done it too. What changed? Not human physiology, but human psychology. Once someone proved it was possible, others believed they could do it too.

This same principle applies in entrepreneurship. When Airbnb launched, the idea of staying in a stranger's home seemed crazy to many. Now it's a multi-billion-dollar industry that's transformed how we travel. The founders' entrepreneurial mindset allowed them to see an opportunity where others saw impossibility.

The Vulnerability Factor: Your Secret Gateway to Authentic Leadership

Now, let's talk about something that doesn't get discussed enough in entrepreneurship: Vulnerability. Brené Brown, a research professor at the University of Houston, has found that vulnerability - the willingness to take emotional risks - is crucial for innovation and creativity.

I will tell you my personal story, as an entrepreneur, I've learned this lesson the hard way. My first podcast appearance taught me a crucial lesson about entrepreneurship. Despite decades of business experience, I found myself gripped by self-doubt and fear of public judgment. The microphone seemed to amplify every insecurity - would my insights resonate? Could I articulate my journey effectively? These moments of vulnerability reminded me that growth often lies just beyond our comfort zone.

But here's the truth: every time I've been vulnerable - shared a personal success story, admitted a mistake, asked for help - it's led to deeper connections with my network and opened up new opportunities.

Vulnerability in leadership doesn't mean being weak. It means having the courage to be yourself, to admit when you don't have all the answers, and to connect authentically with your network, team and customers.

The Truth About Mindset: Your Fears Don't Define You, Your Actions Do

Now, let's get real for a moment. Developing an entrepreneurial mindset isn't about positive affirmations or wishful thinking. It's about-facing hard truths and making tough choices.

Here's a truth bomb for you: your mindset is a choice. Every day, you choose how you respond to challenges, how you interpret failures, and what you believe about your abilities.

And sometimes, choosing a growth mindset feels like crap. It means pushing yourself out of your comfort zone, facing your fears, and doing things that scare you. But you know what? That discomfort is the price of growth. It's the cost of becoming the entrepreneur you're capable of being.

Exercise: Identifying and Challenging Limiting Beliefs

Let's put this into practice right now. Take out a piece of paper and write down three limiting beliefs you have about yourself as an entrepreneur. Maybe it's "I'm not good with numbers" or "I'm not a natural leader" or "I am too old to start a business."

Now, for each belief, ask yourself:

1. Is this belief 100% true, 100% of the time?

2. What evidence do I have that contradicts this belief?
3. How is this belief serving me? How is it holding me back?
4. If this belief weren't true, what would be possible for me?

Finally, rewrite each limiting belief as a growth-oriented statement. For example, "I'm not good with numbers" could become "I'm learning to understand and manage my finances better every day or age is just a number and there are lot of successful entrepreneurs who started at that age."

Remember, changing your mindset is a process. It takes time and consistent effort. But every time you challenge a limiting belief, every time you choose growth over fear, you're rewiring your brain for success.

Action Steps:

1. Start a "Mindset Journal": Each day, write down one limiting belief you encountered and how you challenged it.
2. Create a "Growth Trigger": Choose a physical cue (like a bracelet or a phone wallpaper) to remind you to shift into a growth mindset when faced with challenges.
3. Find an Accountability Partner: Share your mindset goals with someone who can support and challenge you.

Key Takeaways:

- Your mindset shapes your reality as an entrepreneur.
- A growth mindset leads to greater resilience, innovation, and success.
- Vulnerability and authenticity are strengths, not weaknesses, in entrepreneurship.
- Changing your mindset is a choice - a challenging but transformative one.

As we wrap up this chapter, I want you to remember this: the entrepreneurial mindset isn't just about achieving success - it's about who you become in the process. It's about growing, learning, and constantly pushing yourself to new heights.

Your journey as an entrepreneur starts in your mind. So, are you ready to rewire your brain for success? The choice is yours. And I believe in you.

Let's embrace the entrepreneurial mindset. Let's push past our limiting beliefs. Let's be uncomfortable. Your next level of success is waiting on the other side of your mindset paradigm. Go seize it.

Chapter 2

Embracing Failure - Your Steppingstone to Success

> I have not failed. I've just found 10,000 ways that won't work."
> - Thomas Edison

In this chapter I will show you how to transform your relationship with failure by discovering how the world's most successful entrepreneurs use setbacks as catalysts for breakthrough innovation. Through research-backed strategies and real-world examples, learn to reframe failures as essential feedback that guides you toward success. Master the art of 'failing forward' and develop the resilience to turn every setback into a setup for your next big achievement.

In the summer of 1978, a young engineer named James Dyson became frustrated with his Hoover Junior vacuum cleaner. The bag was constantly clogging, causing the suction to drop. Most people would have simply bought a new vacuum. Dyson, however, saw an opportunity.

He set out to create a bagless vacuum that wouldn't lose suction. What followed was a five-year odyssey of failure and persistence that would make even the most stubborn entrepreneur wince. Dyson built 5,126 prototypes, each one a failure, before finally cracking the code with prototype number 5,127.

Let that sink in for a moment. 5,126 failures. Can you imagine the determination it took to keep going after the 100th failure? The 1,000th? The 5,000th? But Dyson persisted, and his eventual success revolutionized the vacuum industry, making him a billionaire in the process.

This, my fellow entrepreneurs, is the power of embracing failure. It's not just about bouncing back from setbacks. It's about recognizing that failure is an integral part of the innovation process, a crucial steppingstone on the path to success. Think about it like a scientist in a laboratory - each failed experiment brings them closer to a breakthrough by eliminating what doesn't work. Every "no" is actually a "know" - valuable data that guides your next attempt. When Thomas Edison was asked about his thousands of failed attempts to create the light bulb, he famously said, "I have not failed. I've just found 10,000 ways that won't work."

This mindset shift is revolutionary: instead of seeing failure as a dead end, you begin to see it as a detour leading to a better route. It's like having a GPS that recalculates your path to success every time you hit a roadblock. The most successful entrepreneurs don't just tolerate failure - they actively seek it out, knowing that each misstep contains the seeds of future success. They understand that in the fast-paced world of business, the real failure isn't in falling - it's in playing it so safe that you never risk falling at all.

The Psychology of Failure: Every Setback is a Setup for Your Comeback

Now, I know what you're thinking. "Kay Kay, it's easy to talk about embracing failure when you're successful. But failing sucks." And you're absolutely right. Failure does suck. It's painful, it's embarrassing, and it can shake your confidence to the core.

But here's where it gets interesting. Dr. Carol Dweck, whose work we explored in the last chapter, has found that our response to failure is deeply tied to our mindset. Those with a fixed mindset see failure as evidence of their limitations. Those with a growth mindset, however, see failure as an opportunity to learn and improve.

In one study, Dweck and her colleagues gave children a series of puzzles to solve. The first few were easy, but the last one was impossible. Children with a fixed mindset quickly became discouraged, with some even saying they were "not smart" after failing. Children with a growth mindset, on the other hand, relished the challenge. One even exclaimed, "I love a challenge!"

The same principle applies in entrepreneurship. A study published in the Journal of Business Venturing found that entrepreneurs who viewed failure as a learning opportunity were more likely to persist in their ventures and ultimately achieve success.

From Setback to Feedback: Reframing Failure

So how do we shift our perspective on failure? It starts with reframing. Instead of seeing failure as a setback, we need to view it as feedback.

Think about it like this: if you're navigating a maze, hitting a dead end isn't a failure. It's valuable information that helps you find the right path. Each "failure" eliminates a possibility, bringing you one step closer to success. Just as a detective uses evidence to narrow down suspects, each dead end in business helps you refine your strategy, sharpen your approach, and deepen your understanding of what works. When you hit a wall in product development, you haven't failed - you've discovered one way your customers don't want to be served. When a marketing campaign flops, you haven't failed - you've gathered priceless data about your audience's preferences. Every setback is like a chisel, sculpting away what doesn't work to reveal the masterpiece of success underneath.

This reframing isn't just a mental trick. It actually changes how our brains process failure. Neuroscientists have found that when we view failure as an opportunity to learn, it activates the regions of our brain associated with growth and skill development. Studies at Stanford University's Neuroscience Institute show that this mindset shift triggers increased activity in the prefrontal cortex - the area responsible for learning and problem-solving. When we embrace failure as feedback, our brains release different neurotransmitters, shifting from the stress chemicals that inhibit learning to the reward chemicals that enhance it. It's like upgrading your brain's operating system from "panic mode" to "learning mode."

Entrepreneurs who master this mental shift often report not just better business outcomes, but also reduced stress, improved creativity, and greater resilience in the face of challenges. Just as an athlete's muscles grow stronger through the stress of exercise, your entrepreneurial capabilities grow stronger through the stress of failure - but only if you view that stress as constructive rather than destructive.

The Unexpected Connection: Failure and Innovation

Now, here's something that might blow your mind: failure isn't just a part of the innovation process - it's often the catalyst for breakthrough innovations.

Take the story of Percy Spencer, an engineer at Raytheon. One day in 1945, Spencer was working with a magnetron, a key component of radar systems. He noticed that the chocolate bar in his pocket had melted. Most people would have been annoyed. Spencer was intrigued.

He started experimenting, trying to heat other foods with the magnetron. Many of his experiments failed, but eventually, these "failures" led to the invention of the microwave oven.

This pattern repeats throughout the history of innovation. Post-It Notes were the result of a failed attempt to create a super-strong adhesive. Viagra was originally developed as a treatment for angina, and its now-famous side effect was initially seen as a failure.

The lesson? Sometimes your biggest failures can lead to your greatest successes - if you're open to the possibilities.

The Vulnerability of Failure: Your Greatest Weakness is Hiding it

Now, let's talk about something that doesn't get discussed enough when it comes to failure: vulnerability. As Brené Brown has pointed out, vulnerability isn't weakness - it's emotional risk-taking, and it's essential for innovation and authentic leadership.

I'll share a personal story. My first podcast interview was a perfect storm of mishaps as I discussed in the last chapter. Despite hours of preparation, my usual business confidence crumbled as audio issues plagued the session and my well-rehearsed answers dissolved into nervous stammers. As a successful real estate investor who routinely handled million-dollar negotiations, I was reduced to a hesitant, rambling novice—even stumbling through my familiar immigrant entrepreneur story. While I initially wanted to bury this mortifying experience, it became a transformative moment in my journey. That "failure" taught me the power of authenticity over perfection and turned into my catalyst for developing genuine media presence and public speaking skills.

In my next podcast appearance, I chose vulnerability by opening with: "My last podcast interview was a complete disaster." Instead of hiding behind perfection, I shared my journey from nervous wreck to finding my authentic voice. The result was unexpected listeners resonated deeply with this honesty, sharing their own stumbles and setbacks. What I learned was profound: vulnerability didn't weaken my credibility; it strengthened it. By admitting my weaknesses, I had inadvertently discovered my greatest strength.

That experience taught me a valuable lesson: being open about your failures doesn't make people lose respect for you. If anything, it makes them trust you more.

The Truth About Failure: It's Not the End, It's the Beginning

Alright, time for some real talk. Here's the truth about failure that most "motivational" speakers won't tell you: failure feels depressing. It's not fun. It's not immediately rewarding. And no matter how many times you experience it, it never stops being painful.

But here's the other truth: failure is inevitable if you're pushing your boundaries and trying to achieve great things. The only way to avoid failure is to play it safe, to never take risks, to stay firmly within your comfort zone. And let's be real - that's not why you became an entrepreneur.

So instead of trying to avoid failure, we need to get comfortable with the failures. We need to recognize that failure is not the opposite of success - it's a crucial part of success.

Think of it like this: failure is to success what working out is to physical fitness. It's uncomfortable, sometimes painful, but it's the stress that forces you to grow stronger.

Leveraging Failure for Future Success: Your Mistakes are Your Most Valuable Assets

So how do successful entrepreneurs leverage failure for future success? Here are some strategies:

1. Conduct a Failure Post-Mortem: After each failure, take time to analyze what went wrong and why. Be brutally honest with yourself. What could you have done that you didn't.

2. Extract the Lessons: Identify the lessons learned from the failure. Identify specific lessons you can apply to future endeavors. These lessons are the silver lining of your failure.

3. Adjust and Iterate: Use the insights from your failure to refine your approach. Remember, Edison didn't create 10,000 separate inventions - he made 10,000 iterations of the same invention.

4. Share Your Failures: Declaring openly about your failures not only helps you process them but can also provide valuable insights to others.

5. Celebrate the Attempt: Recognize that each failure represents an effort, a risk taken. That's something to be proud of, regardless of the outcome.

Exercise: Start Your Failure Resume

Now, let's put this into practice. I want you to start what I call a "Failure Resume." This isn't about dwelling on your failures - it's about extracting value from them.

Here's how to do it:

1. List Your Recent Failures: Write down 3-5 recent failures in your entrepreneurial journey.

2. Analyze Each Failure: For each failure, answer these questions:
   - What was the goal?
   - What went wrong?
   - What factors contributed to the failure?
   - What did I learn from this experience?
   - How can I apply this lesson in the future?

3. Identify Patterns: Look at your failures collectively. Do you see any patterns? Are there recurring issues you need to address?

4. Plan for the Future: Based on your analysis, lessons learned from failures, what specific actions can you take to improve your chances of success in the future?

Remember, this isn't a one-time exercise. Make it a habit to update your Failure Resume regularly. Over time, you'll start to see your failures not as setbacks, but as a record of your growth and learning.

Action Steps:

1. Start Your Failure Resume: Use the exercise above to create and maintain your Failure Resume.
2. Practice Reframing: Next time you experience a failure, consciously practice reframing it as feedback. What did this experience teach you?
3. Share a Failure Story: Challenge yourself to openly share a story of failure with your team or peers. Focus on what you learned and how it made you better.

Key Takeaways:

- Failure is not the opposite of success - it's one of the crucial parts of the success process.
- Reframing failure as feedback can change how our brains process and learn from setbacks.
- Being vulnerable about our failures can strengthen trust and authenticity in leadership.
- Systematically analyzing and learning from failures is key to leveraging them for future success.

As we conclude this chapter, I want you to remember this: your relationship with failure will largely determine your success as an entrepreneur. It's not about avoiding failure - it's about failing forward, learning fast, and using each setback as a springboard for your entrepreneurial growth.

So, are you ready to embrace failure as your teacher? Are you prepared to see each setback as a step forward? The choice is yours. And I believe in you.

Let's redefine our relationship with failure. Let's turn our setbacks into comebacks. Your next big breakthrough might be waiting on the other side of your next failure. Go find it.

Chapter 3

The Vision Quest - Crafting Your Entrepreneurial Dream

> The only thing worse than being blind is having sight but no vision."
> - Helen Keller

In this chapter you will learn how to transform your entrepreneurial dreams into a clear, compelling vision that drives success and inspires others. Discover science-backed techniques to not just visualize your future, but to create a practical roadmap that turns aspirations into achievements. Master the art of visionary leadership while staying grounded in practical execution, combining the power of imagination with strategic action.

It was 1994, and Jeff Bezos was comfortably employed at a prestigious Wall Street firm, where he had become the youngest senior vice president in the company's history. His future was secure, his path to wealth and success clearly mapped out. But something was nagging at him - a statistic that internet usage was growing at 2,300% per year. Most people would have found this interesting and moved on, filed it away as a curious fact at a cocktail party. Bezos saw a vision of the future, a glimpse of a world that didn't exist yet but could.

He imagined a world where people could buy anything online, where selection was infinite, and prices were transparent. He envisioned a digital marketplace that would break down geographical barriers, where a person in a small rural town could access the same products as someone in New York City. It was a radical idea at a time when most people were still figuring out how to use email, and when the idea of entering your credit card information online seemed like madness. But Bezos' vision was so compelling that he was willing to leave his secure job and take a massive risk. He wrote his business plan while driving cross-country to Seattle with his wife MacKenzie, choosing the city for its large pool of tech talent and proximity to a major book wholesaler.

Fast forward to today, and Amazon is one of the most valuable companies in the world, having revolutionized not just retail, but cloud computing, entertainment, and more. The company that started in a garage selling books has transformed how we shop, how businesses operate, and even how we consume media. Prime delivery has made two-day shipping the standard. AWS powers a vast portion of the internet. Alexa sits in millions of homes. All because one man had a vision and the courage to pursue it, even when critics called Amazon "Amazon.bomb" during the dot-com crash.

This, my fellow entrepreneurs, is the power of vision. It's not just about having a good idea or spotting a market opportunity. It's about seeing a future that doesn't exist yet and having the audacity to believe you can make it real. Vision is like a powerful magnet that pulls you forward when doubts creep in, when obstacles arise, when others say it can't be done. It's the force that keeps you working in your garage when others are comfortable in their corner offices. It's what transforms seemingly crazy ideas into world-changing realities. A true vision isn't just a goal or a business plan - it's a deeply held conviction about what's possible, combined with the courage to act on that conviction, even when the path forward isn't clear.

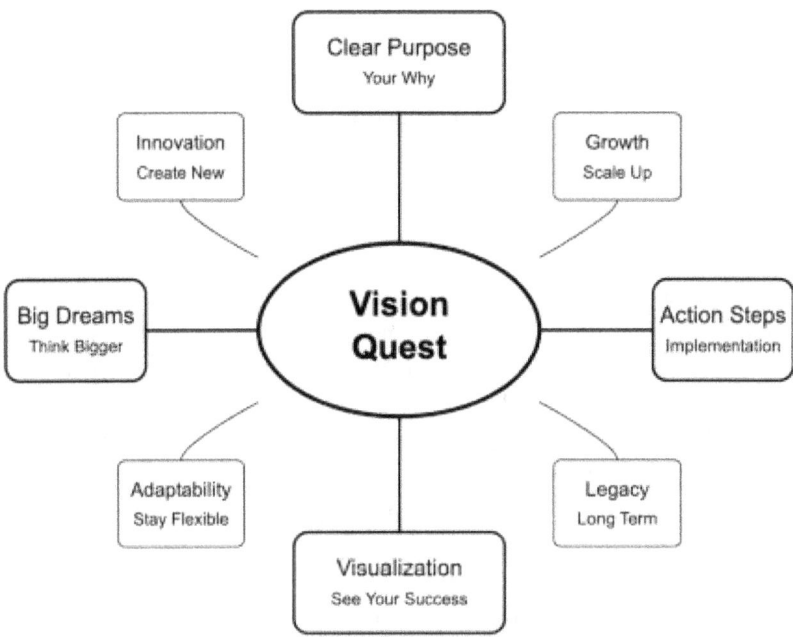

The Science of Vision: What Your Eyes Can See, Your Mind Can Achieve

Now, you might be thinking, "Kay Kay, that's a nice story, but what does it have to do with me?" Well, here's where it gets interesting. The power of vision isn't just anecdotal - it's backed by hard science.

Dr. Gabriele Oettingen, a psychology professor at New York University, has spent decades studying the science of goal achievement. Her research has shown that people who vividly imagine their desired future are significantly more likely to achieve their goals.

In one study, Oettingen and her colleagues found that students who visualized themselves succeeding academically and contrasted this with their current reality were more likely to earn higher grades than those who didn't engage in this visualization exercise.

But here's the kicker: it's not just about positive thinking. Oettingen's research shows that the most effective approach is what she calls "mental contrasting" - vividly imagining your desired future, then comparing it with your current reality. This process helps you identify obstacles and develop strategies to overcome them.

For entrepreneurs, this means not just dreaming big, but also being realistic about the challenges you'll face. It's about having a clear vision of where you want to go, while also understanding where you are now and what it will take to bridge that gap. Think of it like planning a cross-country journey - yes, you need to know your destination, but you also need to understand your starting point, the terrain you'll cross, the resources you'll need, and the obstacles you might encounter along the way.

This pragmatic approach to vision doesn't mean limiting your dreams - quite the opposite. It means breaking down those big dreams into actionable steps, understanding the skills you'll need to develop, the resources you'll need to acquire, and the partnerships you'll need to build. It's about being both a dreamer and a doer, combining the ability to see what's possible with the practical wisdom to make it happen.

The Unexpected Connection: Vision and Neuroplasticity

Now, let's dive a bit deeper into the brain. Neuroscientists have discovered that our brains are incredibly plastic - they can change and rewire themselves based on our thoughts and experiences.

When we consistently focus on a vision, we're actually creating new neural pathways in our brains. It's like we're carving out a roadmap for our future success.

Think about it like this: have you ever bought a new car and suddenly started noticing that same model everywhere? That's because you've primed your brain to recognize it. In the same way, when you have a clear vision for your business, you start noticing opportunities and resources that align with that vision.

This principle doesn't just apply to business. In the world of sports, athletes use visualization techniques to improve their performance. A study of Olympic athletes found that 70-90% of them used visualization as part of their training.

Imagine a basketball player visualizing the perfect free throw. They're not just daydreaming - they're actually strengthening the neural pathways associated with that action. When it comes time to perform in real life, their brain already has a blueprint for success.

As entrepreneurs, we can use this same principle. By regularly visualizing our business success, we're training our brains to recognize and seize opportunities that align with our vision.

Crafting Your Entrepreneurial Vision: The Clearer Your Picture, The Stronger Your Purpose

So, how do we actually create a compelling vision for our businesses? Let's break it down into actionable steps:

- Start with Your Why: Before you think about what you want to achieve, connect with why it matters to you. What impact do you want to have on the world?
- Think Big, Then Think Bigger: Don't limit yourself based on what seems "realistic." Remember, every world-changing innovation started as an "unrealistic" vision.
- Make It Vivid: Use all your senses when visualizing your future. What does success look, feel, sound, and even smell like?

- Write It Down: There's power in putting pen to paper. Write out your vision in detail. Make it so real you can almost touch it.
- Create a Vision Board: Use images, words, and symbols to create a visual representation of your vision. Keep it somewhere you'll see it every time, every day.
- Share It: Articulate your vision to others. This not only makes it more real for you but can also attract people who resonate with your vision.
- Open Declaration: Declare your vision to your family, friends, collogues and to the world and share it on social media.

The Vulnerability of Vision: The Bigger Your Dreams, The More Courage They Demand

Now, let's talk about something that often gets overlooked when discussing vision - vulnerability. Sharing your vision can be scary. It opens you up to criticism, skepticism, and the possibility of failure.

I'll share a personal story from my early days. When I launched my travel agency in India, the skepticism was overwhelming. Industry veterans dismissed my ambitions, friends questioned my judgment, and even my parents pleaded with me to pursue a "sensible" corporate career. The market was indeed crowded with established agencies, and as a young entrepreneur, I faced the double challenge of inexperience and fierce competition. But sometimes, the loudest voices of doubt become the strongest fuel for determination. Looking back, those early skeptics inadvertently shaped my resilience and innovative approach to other businesses.

It was tempting to keep my vision to myself, to play it safe. But I realized that by being vulnerable and sharing my vision, I was also opening myself up to support, collaboration, and opportunities.

Being vulnerable with your vision doesn't mean being naive or ignoring potential obstacles. It means being authentic about your dreams and your fears and inviting others to be part of your journey.

Chapter 3: The Vision Quest - Crafting Your Entrepreneurial Dream

The Truth About Vision: Faith in The Invisible Creates the Visible

Alright, time for some real talk. Here's the truth about vision that most people won't tell you: having a vision doesn't guarantee success. It's not a magic spell that will make all your dreams come true. Just like having a map doesn't automatically get you to your destination, having a vision alone won't build your empire. Some of the most passionate visionaries I've met are still dreaming because they never translated their vision into concrete action. Walt Disney himself said, "The way to get started is to quit talking and begin doing."

But here's the other truth: not having a vision pretty much guarantees that you won't achieve extraordinary success. Without a clear vision, you're like a ship without a destination - you might stay afloat, but you're not going anywhere specific. You'll find yourself reacting to circumstances rather than creating them, chasing other people's dreams instead of pursuing your own. Look at any great business success story - from Steve Jobs revolutionizing personal computing to Sara Blakely transforming the shapewear industry with Spanx - they all started with a clear, compelling vision of what could be.

Your vision is your North Star. It guides your decisions, motivates you during tough times, and attracts the right people and opportunities to you. But it's not enough on its own. You need to pair it with action, persistence, and a willingness to adapt as you go. Vision without execution is hallucination, as Thomas Edison famously said. I've seen too many entrepreneurs fall in love with their vision but fail to do the unglamorous daily work needed to make it reality. Your vision might be to build a real estate empire, but are you willing to make those hundred cold calls a day?

Aligning Vision with Values: Success Without Purpose Is Just Expensive Failure

One crucial aspect of crafting a powerful vision is ensuring it aligns with your core values and purpose. A vision that conflicts with your values is like trying to row a boat against the current - you might make progress, but it'll be exhausting and unsustainable.

Take the example of Patagonia founder Yvon Chouinard. His vision wasn't just to build a successful outdoor clothing company, but to prove that a business could be environmentally responsible and still be profitable. This vision aligned perfectly with his personal values and has guided Patagonia's decisions for decades.

Exercise: Crafting Your Vision Board

Now, let's put this into practice with a vision board exercise. This isn't just about cutting out pretty pictures from magazines. It's about creating a powerful visual representation of your entrepreneurial future.
Here's how to do it:

1. Gather Your Materials: Get a large poster board, magazines, scissors, glue, and markers or if you want to make it digital, I use Canva to make my vision boards.

2. Clarify Your Vision: Before you start, spend some time thinking about your vision. What do you want to achieve? How do you want to impact the world? What does success look like to you? Where are you now and where you want to go?

3. Find Representative Images: Look for images that represent different aspects of your vision. This could include pictures of your ideal workspace, symbols of success, the places you want to visit or images that represent the impact you want to have.

4. Add Words and Phrases: Include powerful words or phrases that resonate with your vision like Work Hard Dream Big. These could be your core values, your mission statement, or motivational quotes.

Chapter 3: The Vision Quest - Crafting Your Entrepreneurial Dream

5. Arrange and Glue: Arrange your images and words on the board or a digital board in a way that feels right to you. There's no wrong way to do this - it's your vision.

6. Add Personal Touches: Consider adding personal elements like photos of yourself or your family or your team, or symbols that have special meaning to you.

7. Display Prominently: Put your vision board somewhere you'll see it every day. The more you engage with it, the more powerful it becomes.

Remember, this isn't a one-time exercise. Your vision may evolve over time, and that's okay. The important thing is to keep it front and center in your mind. I make it once a year and make changes as important new goals come my way.

Action Steps:

1. Create Your Vision Board: Use the exercise above to create a powerful visual representation of your entrepreneurial vision.
2. Daily Visualization Practice: Spend 5-10 minutes each day visualizing your success. Make it as vivid and detailed as possible. Assess where you are in the process of achieving those goals.
3. Share Your Vision: Challenge yourself to articulate your vision to at least three people this week. Pay attention to how it evolves as you share it.

Key Takeaways:

- A clear, compelling vision is crucial for entrepreneurial success.
- Visualization is a scientifically proven technique for goal achievement.
- Vulnerability in sharing your vision can lead to unexpected opportunities and support.
- Your vision should align with your core values and purpose for sustainable success.

As we wrap up this chapter, I want you to remember this: your vision is not just a nice-to-have. It's the foundation of your entrepreneurial journey. It's what will keep you going when things get tough, guide your decisions when you're faced with choices, and inspire others to join you on your mission.

So, are you ready to craft a vision that excites and challenges you? Are you prepared to see a future that doesn't exist yet and commit to making it real? The choice is yours. And I believe in you.

Let's dream big. Let's craft visions that scare us a little bit. Your next level of success is waiting on the other side of your boldest vision. Go create it.

Chapter 4

Building Resilience - Your Entrepreneurial Armor

> It's not that I'm so smart, it's just that I stay with problems longer."
> - Albert Einstein

In this chapter you will discover how to build unshakeable resilience that transforms challenges from obstacles into opportunities for growth. Through proven psychological frameworks and real-world entrepreneurial examples, learn to develop your emotional and mental fortitude in the face of setbacks. Master the art of bouncing back stronger from every challenge, building an entrepreneurial armor that not only protects you but propels you forward.

In 1995, a young entrepreneur named Howard Schultz faced a pivotal moment that would test his resilience. Starbucks, the company he had built from a small Seattle coffee shop into a growing chain, was experiencing a major crisis. Sales were plummeting, customer complaints were rising, and the company's ambitious expansion plans seemed to be backfiring. The very core of what made Starbucks special - the quality of its coffee and the customer experience - was being compromised in the rush to grow.

Many advised Schultz to slow down the expansion, cut costs, and lower quality standards to improve profitability. Instead, he made a bold and counterintuitive decision. He temporarily closed 7,100 U.S. stores for several hours to retrain 135,000 baristas on how to make the perfect espresso. Wall Street analysts called it financial suicide. The move would cost the company an estimated $6 million in lost revenue, and many questioned whether customers would even notice the difference.

But Schultz wasn't just thinking about the bottom line. He was focused on the company's resilience and long-term success. "We had to take a big step back to take a big step forward," he explained. This decision demonstrated the kind of resilience that separates great entrepreneurs from good ones - the ability to make tough choices that prioritize long-term sustainability over short-term gains.

The results? The retraining initiative not only improved coffee quality but also reinvigorated employee morale and customer loyalty. In the years that followed, Starbucks emerged stronger than ever, expanding globally while maintaining its commitment to quality and culture.

This, my fellow entrepreneurs, is the power of resilience. It's not just about weathering storms - it's about using challenges as catalysts for transformation. It's about having the courage to make difficult decisions when everyone else is telling you to take the easy way out.

The Psychology of Resilience: Your Scars Tell the Story of Your Strength

Now, you might be thinking, Kay Kay, that's a great story, but what if I'm just not naturally resilient?" Well, here's some good news: resilience isn't a fixed trait. It's a skill that can be developed and strengthened over time.

Dr. Angela Duckworth, a psychologist at the University of Pennsylvania, has spent years studying what she calls "grit" - the combination of passion and perseverance that allows some people to achieve long-term goals while others give up.

In her research, Duckworth found that grit was a better predictor of success than IQ, talent, or any other factor. But here's the crucial part: grit isn't something you're born with. It's something you can cultivate.

One study by Duckworth and her colleagues followed cadets at West Point Military Academy. They found that cadets who scored high on the "grit scale" were 60% more likely to complete the grueling summer training program than their peers, regardless of other factors like athletic ability or academic achievement.

The same principle applies in entrepreneurship. A study published in the Journal of Business Venturing found that entrepreneurs with higher levels of resilience were more likely to persist in their ventures and ultimately achieve success.

The Unexpected Connection: Resilience and Creativity

Now, let's dive into something that might surprise you: resilience isn't just about gritting your teeth and pushing through hardship. It's actually your secret weapon for unlocking creativity and innovation in business. This connection isn't just motivational fluff - it's backed by solid research and proven through countless entrepreneurial success stories.

Think about it like this: when you're resilient, you're able to stay with problems longer. You don't pack up and go home at the first sign of difficulty, or even the tenth. You stick around when others have long since thrown in the towel. And here's where the magic happens - in that extra time, in those additional attempts, in those moments when most people would have quit, your brain starts forming new neural pathways. You begin seeing connections that weren't visible before. Solutions emerge from unexpected places.

Let me paint this picture with a real-world example. When Walt Disney was trying to synchronize sound with animation for "Steamboat Willie" in 1928, he failed repeatedly. Most people would have settled for silent cartoons - they were profitable enough. But Disney's resilience kept him experimenting, tinkering, and pushing boundaries. The result? He revolutionized animation and created an entertainment empire that has shaped popular culture for nearly a century.

This isn't just about having a never-give-up attitude. It's about understanding that resilience creates a psychological safety net that allows your creativity to take bigger risks. When you know you can bounce back from failure, you're more willing to try bold, innovative solutions. You're more likely to ask, "what if?" instead of settling for "what is."

Think of resilience as your creativity's insurance policy. It gives you the confidence to venture into uncharted territory, to experiment with unconventional ideas, to push past the obvious solutions to find something truly groundbreaking. Every time you pick yourself up after a setback, you're not just showing toughness - you're building your creative muscles.

And here's where it gets really interesting: this resilience-creativity loop becomes self-reinforcing. Each creative breakthrough boosts your resilience, making you more likely to persist through the next challenge. Each display of resilience expands your creative capacity, enabling you to envision even more innovative solutions.

The lesson? Sometimes your greatest innovations come after your biggest setbacks - if you have the resilience to keep going.

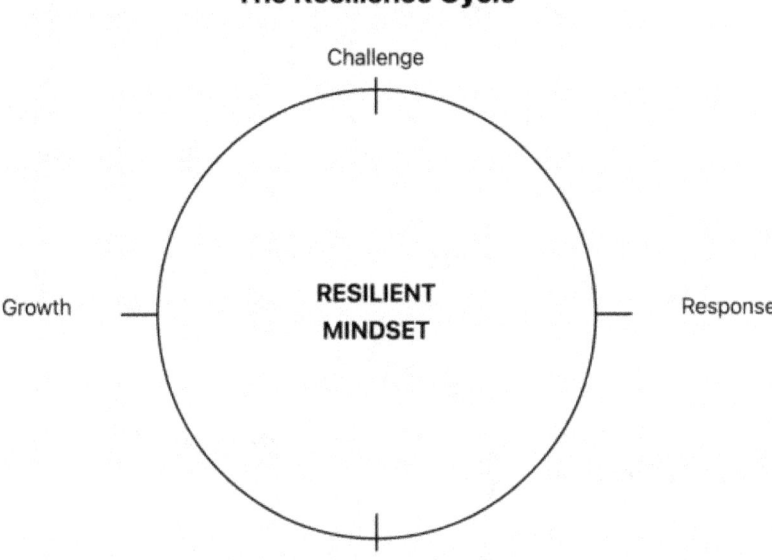

Strategies for Developing Mental Toughness

So, how do we actually build this crucial skill of resilience? Let's break it down into actionable steps:

1. Reframe Setbacks: Instead of seeing failures as end of the tunnel, view them as learning opportunities. Ask yourself, "What can I learn from this?"

2. Practice Mindfulness: Mindfulness meditation has been shown to increase resilience by helping you manage stress and stay focused on the present.

3. Build a Support Network: Surround yourself with people who believe in you and can offer support during tough times.

4. Set Realistic Goals: Break big goals into smaller, achievable steps. This allows you to experience regular wins, building your confidence and resilience.

5. Take Care of Your Physical Health: Exercise, good nutrition, and adequate sleep all contribute to mental resilience.

6. Develop a Growth Mindset: Remember Carol Dweck's work from earlier chapters? A growth mindset is crucial for resilience.

7. Practice Self-Compassion: Be kind to yourself when you face setbacks. Treat yourself with the same compassion you'd offer a good friend.

The Vulnerability Factor: The Transformative Power of Authenticity

Now, let's talk about something that doesn't get discussed enough when it comes to resilience: vulnerability. As Brené Brown has pointed out, vulnerability isn't weakness - it's actually a sign of courage and strength.

I'll share a pivotal moment from my entrepreneurial journey that fundamentally shaped my understanding of authentic leadership. In 2009, I faced a critical challenge with my ground-up gas station development. Despite having experience operating multiple successful stations, this new venture presented unexpected hurdles - the modern facilities and prime location weren't generating the anticipated traffic, resulting in negative cash flow month after month. Initially, I attempted to maintain what I thought was a "professional" facade, masking our challenges behind a veneer of unwavering confidence and projected success.

This approach, while aligned with traditional notions of entrepreneurial strength, proved counterproductive. The energy spent maintaining this image not only drained valuable resources but created an invisible barrier between myself and my partners.

It hindered authentic connections with customers who could have provided valuable feedback, partners who might have offered strategic insights.

The real transformation began when I shifted from projecting an image of perfection to embracing transparent leadership. By acknowledging our challenges openly and engaging genuinely with the partners, we not only gained valuable insights that helped turn the business around but also built lasting relationships that proved instrumental to our long-term success. This experience taught me that true entrepreneurial strength lies not in appearing infallible, but in having the courage to lead with authenticity and vulnerability.

The Truth About Resilience: Life Will Break You, But You Choose How You Repair

Alright, time for some real talk. Here's the truth about resilience that most people won't tell you, and it might just flip your whole understanding of what being "tough" really means: resilience isn't about never feeling discouraged or wanting to quit. It's about feeling those things - really feeling them - and pushing forward anyway. It's about standing in the storm of self-doubt, fear, and uncertainty, acknowledging these feelings, and still taking that next step forward.

Let me be crystal clear here: if you're waiting to feel invincible before taking action, you'll be waiting forever. I've met countless entrepreneurs who think they're "doing it wrong" because they feel scared, discouraged, or overwhelmed. They see other successful business leaders and assume these people never experience doubt or fear. But here's the reality check - everyone feels these things. The difference is that resilient entrepreneurs have learned to coexist with these feelings rather than being paralyzed by them.

Resilience isn't the absence of difficulty - it's the ability to persist in the face of it. It's not about being unbreakable; it's about being able to put yourself back together after you've been broken. Sometimes it's about gathering those broken pieces and building something even stronger than before. Think of the Japanese art of Kintsugi, where broken pottery is repaired with gold, making the piece more beautiful and valuable than the original. That's what true resilience looks like in entrepreneurship.

Think of it like this: resilience is like a muscle. You don't build muscle by avoiding stress - you build it by exposing yourself to stress and then recovering. The same is true for resilience. Each setback, each failure, each moment of doubt is an opportunity to strengthen your resilience muscle. Just like in the gym, growth happens during recovery, not during the stress itself. This is why reflection and learning from challenges are just as important as facing them.

So, here's your wake-up call: stop waiting to feel ready. Stop waiting for the fear to go away. Stop beating yourself up for having moments of doubt. Instead, start seeing these challenges for what they really are - opportunities to strengthen your resilience muscle. Embrace the discomfort of growth. Welcome the resistance that makes you stronger.

Remember: the goal isn't to be unbreakable. The goal is to become increasingly skillful at putting yourself back together, learning from each experience, and coming back stronger than before. That's not just resilience - that's the very essence of entrepreneurial growth.

But here's the key: just like physical exercise, building resilience requires consistent practice. You can't just read about it or think about it - you must actively work on it every day.

Exercise: Develop Your Personal Resilience Ritual

Now, let's put this into practice with a personal resilience ritual. This is a set of actions you'll take whenever you face a setback or challenge. The goal is to help you process the difficulty, learn from it, and bounce back stronger.

Here's how to create your ritual:

1. Acknowledge the Setback: Start by simply acknowledging what happened. Don't try to minimize it or pretend it doesn't bother you.

2. Feel Your Emotions: Allow yourself to feel whatever emotions come up - frustration, disappointment, anger. Set a timer for 5 minutes and let yourself fully experience these feelings.

3. Practice Self-Compassion: Speak to yourself kindly, as you would to a good friend facing a similar situation.

4. Extract the Lesson: Ask yourself, "What can I learn from this experience? How can I use this to grow stronger or smarter?"

5. Visualize Overcoming: Spend a few minutes visualizing yourself overcoming this challenge and achieving your goals.

6. Take One Small Action: Identify one small step you can take immediately to move forward and do it.

7. Express Gratitude: End your ritual by noting three things you're grateful for, even during this challenge.

Customize this ritual to what works best for you. The important thing is to have a consistent practice that helps you process setbacks and bounce back stronger.

Action Steps

1. Create Your Resilience Ritual: Use the exercise above to develop your personal resilience ritual.
2. Practice Daily Resilience: Identify one small challenge each day and practice using your resilience skills to overcome it.
3. Share Your Resilience Story: Challenge yourself to share a story of resilience with someone this week. It could be a personal story or one that inspired you.

Key Takeaways:

- Resilience is a skill that can be developed, not a fixed trait.
- Resilience is closely linked to creativity and innovation in business.
- Vulnerability and authenticity play crucial roles in building true resilience.
- Consistent practice is key to strengthening your resilience "muscle".

As we conclude this chapter, I want you to remember this: your resilience is your entrepreneurial armor. It's what will protect you from the slings and arrows of setbacks and failures. It's what will allow you to keep pushing forward when others would give up.

But unlike physical armor, which shields you from harm, your resilience armor allows you to absorb challenges, learn from them, and come back stronger. It doesn't prevent you from getting knocked down - it ensures that you always get back up.

So, are you ready to build your resilience armor? Are you prepared to face challenges head-on and use them as fuel for your growth? The choice is yours. And I believe in you.

Let's build that resilience. Let's turn our setbacks into comebacks. Your next level of success is waiting on the other side of your next challenge. Go meet it head-on.

Chapter 5

The Growth Mindset Revolution - Unleashing Your Potential

> In a growth mindset, challenges are exciting rather than threatening. So rather than thinking, oh, I'm going to reveal my weaknesses, you say, wow, here's a chance to grow."
> - Carol S. Dweck

In this chapter you'll learn how to unlock the transformative power of the growth mindset and discover how this revolutionary approach can exponentially expand your entrepreneurial capabilities. Learn how successful entrepreneurs use this mindset to turn challenges into learning opportunities and limitations into launching pads for innovation. Master practical techniques to rewire your thinking patterns, moving from 'I can't' to 'I can't yet,' and unleash your full potential for success.

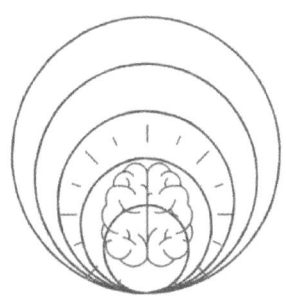

In 2014, Microsoft stood at a critical crossroads. The tech giant that had once dominated the digital landscape with the swagger of an unbeatable champion now resembled a sluggish heavyweight past its prime. The company that had put "a computer on every desk" was being outmaneuvered by nimbler competitors like Apple, Google, and Amazon. Innovation seemed to have abandoned the halls of Redmond, Washington. Employee morale was sinking, and Wall Street had all but written Microsoft off as a relic of the past.

Enter Satya Nadella, a 22-year Microsoft veteran who understood something profound about transformation. Unlike many incoming CEOs who might have launched flashy initiatives or announced dramatic restructuring plans, Nadella's first move was surprisingly subtle yet incredibly powerful. Instead of focusing on products or profits, he zeroed in on something more fundamental: mindset.

In what would prove to be a defining moment, Nadella handed out copies of Carol Dweck's book "Mindset" to his senior leadership team. This wasn't just recommended reading – it was a declaration of cultural revolution.

But Nadella didn't stop there. He systematically dismantled the walls of the old Microsoft culture brick by brick. He encouraged experimentation, explicitly stating that learning from failure was more valuable than avoiding it. In perhaps his boldest move, he pushed for collaboration with competitors – a concept that would have been heretical in the Gates and Ballmer eras. Microsoft began forming partnerships with Linux (once considered Microsoft's arch-nemesis), released Office for iPad, and opened its arms to open-source development.

The results were nothing short of spectacular. Within five years, Microsoft's stock price had tripled, but the real transformation ran much deeper than market capitalization. The company regained its position as an innovation leader, making ambitious moves in cloud computing with Azure, pushing boundaries in artificial intelligence, and pioneering mixed reality with HoloLens.

But here's the real kicker: this transformation wasn't about implementing new policies or restructuring departments. It was about fundamentally changing how people thought about their own potential and the potential of those around them. Nadella had grasped something crucial about organizational change: before you can transform a company's products, processes, or profits, you must first transform its mindset.

This, my fellow entrepreneurs, is the true power of the growth mindset. It's not just some feel-good management theory or self-help concept. It's a fundamental shift in how you view challenges, setbacks, and human potential. It's about replacing "I can't" with "I can't yet," "That's impossible" with "How might we?" and "That's not my job" with "Let me learn about that."

The Science of Growth Mindset: Every Challenge Is Just a Skill You Haven't Mastered Yet

Now, you might be thinking, "Kay Kay, this sounds great, but is there any real evidence behind it?" Absolutely. Let's dive into the science.

Dr. Carol Dweck, a psychology professor at Stanford University, has spent decades researching the impact of mindset on success. Her groundbreaking work has identified two primary mindsets: fixed and growth.

Those with a fixed mindset believe their abilities are static - they're either born with certain talents or they're not. In contrast, those with a growth mindset believe their abilities can be developed through dedication and hard work.

In one study, Dweck and her colleagues followed hundreds of students transitioning to junior high school, a challenging time for many. They found that students with a growth mindset - those who believed their intelligence could be developed - outperformed those with a fixed mindset, even when they entered with equal academic achievement.

But here's where it gets really interesting for us entrepreneurs: this same principle applies in the business world. A study published in the Harvard Business Review found that employees in growth mindset companies are:

- 47% more likely to say their colleagues are trustworthy
- 34% more likely to feel a strong sense of ownership and commitment to the company
- 65% more likely to say that the company supports risk-taking
- 49% more likely to say that the company fosters innovation

The Unexpected Connection: Growth Mindset and Neuroplasticity

Now, let's dive a bit deeper into the brain. Neuroscientists have discovered that our brains are incredibly plastic - they can change and rewire themselves based on our experiences and beliefs.

When we adopt a growth mindset, we're actually changing the physical structure of our brains. We're creating new neural pathways that make learning and adaptation easier over time.

The same principle applies in entrepreneurship. When you approach challenges with a growth mindset, you're not just changing your attitude - you're literally rewiring your brain to be better at learning, problem-solving, and innovation.

Cultivating a Growth Mindset: Your Greatest Enemy Isn't Failure, it's "I Already Know"

So, how do we actually develop a growth mindset? Let's break it down into actionable steps:

1. Embrace Challenges: Instead of avoiding difficult situations, seek them out. Each challenge is an opportunity to grow.

2. Persist in the Face of Setbacks: Remember, failure is not the opposite of success - it's part of success. When you hit a roadblock, ask yourself, "What can I learn from this?"

3. See Effort as the Path to Mastery: Hard work isn't just a means to an end - it's how you develop your abilities and achieve your goals.

4. Learn from Criticism: Don't take feedback personally. Instead, use it as valuable information to improve.

5. Find Lessons and Inspiration in Others' Success: Rather than feeling jealous or threatened by others' achievements, use them as motivation and learning opportunities.

The Vulnerability Factor: Transforming Self-Doubt into Strategic Growth

Now, let's talk about something that doesn't get discussed enough when it comes to growth mindset: vulnerability. As Brené Brown has pointed out, vulnerability isn't weakness - it's the birthplace of innovation, creativity, and change.

I'll share a personal story. When I first stepped onto the stage to discuss multifamily investment benefits in front of hundreds of potential investors, my carefully memorized script felt like a prison. Despite knowing my subject matter—having successfully invested and managed numerous apartment properties and generated consistent returns—I found myself robotically reciting statistics and stumbling over rehearsed phrases. I am sure, the audience could sense my discomfort.

Things changed when I decided to speak from experience rather than from memorized script. I started sharing real stories about how we turned around struggling properties, the mistakes we made in my early investments, and the actual challenges of asset management. When I admitted that my first multifamily deal almost fell apart because we overlooked crucial due diligence steps, the audience leaned in. By being vulnerable about my journey—the successes and the setbacks—I built genuine connections. My presentations became conversations rather than lectures, and surprisingly, this authenticity led to more investors to the audience than my polished pitch ever did.

Embracing a growth mindset means being willing to be vulnerable - to try things you're not good at yet, to ask questions, to admit mistakes. It's not always comfortable, but it's where the real growth happens.

The Truth About Growth Mindset: The Expert Was Once a Beginner Who Refused to Give Up

Alright, time for some real talk. Here's the truth about growth mindset that most people won't tell you: it's not always sunshine and rainbows. In fact, most of the time, real growth feels downright uncomfortable, challenging, and sometimes even terrifying. It's like that moment when you're about to step on stage in front of a huge audience, or when you're about to make that high-stakes business decision – your stomach is in knots, your mind is racing, and everything in you wants to retreat to safety.

Growth mindset doesn't mean you'll always feel confident or that learning will always be fun. That's a myth that needs to be shattered. Sometimes it means pushing through when you feel like an impostor – like when you're sitting in a room full of successful entrepreneurs, and your inner voice is screaming that you don't belong there. Sometimes it means failing publicly and getting back up, like when your new product launch falls flat, and you must face your team the next day. Sometimes it means admitting you were wrong and changing course, even when your ego is begging you to stick to your guns just to save face.

But here's the thing: that discomfort? That pain? That feeling of being completely out of your depth? That's where the magic happens. That's where you're stretching your abilities, rewiring your brain, becoming a better version of yourself. It's in these moments of maximum discomfort that your greatest transformations occur. Every time you push through that wall of self-doubt, every time you choose to learn from failure rather than be defeated by it, you're literally reshaping your neural pathways and expanding your capabilities.

Think of it like working out. The burn you feel in your muscles. That's not a sign that you're weak. It's a sign that you're getting stronger. When you're doing those last few reps, when your muscles are screaming for you to stop, that's precisely when the growth is happening. The same is true for the discomfort that comes with adopting a growth mindset. When you're struggling to understand a new concept, when you're fumbling through a new skill, when you're picking yourself up after a failure – that's not a sign that you're failing. It's a sign that you're growing, evolving, and transforming into something more than you were before.

But here's the secret that successful entrepreneurs know: this discomfort is not your enemy. It's your compass. When you're feeling that resistance, that fear, that uncertainty – you're probably heading in exactly the right direction. Because growth happens at the edge of your comfort zone, not in the safe, cozy center of it.

The Ripple Effect of Growth Mindset: Change Yourself, and Watch the World Change with You

Here's something fascinating about growth mindset: it's contagious. When you adopt a growth mindset, it doesn't just affect you - it influences your entire team and organization.

In a study of seven Fortune 500 companies, researchers found that in organizations with a growth mindset culture, employees reported feeling more empowered and committed. They were also more likely to say their company fostered innovation.

This ripple effect can transform your entire business. It leads to more innovation, better problem-solving, and a more adaptive organization overall. In today's fast-changing business landscape, this can be the difference between thriving and becoming obsolete.

Exercise: Reframing Challenge Through a Growth Mindset Lens

Now, let's put this into practice. I want you to think of a recent challenge or setback you've faced in your business. Got it? Okay, now let's reframe it through the lens of a growth mindset.

1. Describe the Challenge: Write down what happened and how you initially felt about it.

2. Identify Fixed Mindset Thoughts: What thoughts did you have that reflect a fixed mindset? (e.g., "I'm not good at this," "This proves I'm not cut out for entrepreneurship," I cannot do it")

3. Challenge These Thoughts: For each fixed mindset thought, ask yourself: Is this really true? What evidence do I have to the contrary?

4. Reframe with Growth Mindset: Now, rewrite your thoughts from a growth mindset perspective. (e.g., "This is challenging, but it's an opportunity to learn," "I'm not good at this yet, but I can improve with practice and can do it")

5. Identify Learning Opportunities: What can you learn from this challenge? How can you use it to grow?

6. Plan Next Steps: Based on this reframing, what actions can you take to move forward?

Remember, the goal isn't to pretend challenges aren't difficult. It's to approach them as opportunities for growth rather than as threats or final verdicts on your abilities.

Action Steps:

1. Mindset Audit: For the next week, pay attention to your thoughts. When you notice a fixed mindset thought, pause and reframe it from a growth mindset perspective.
2. Embrace a New Challenge: Identify one area of your business where you've been playing it safe. Challenge yourself to try something new or difficult in this area.
3. Create a "Yet" Board: Write down skills or achievements you're working towards, phrasing them with "yet." (e.g., "I'm not profitable yet," "I haven't mastered digital marketing yet") Display this prominently as a reminder of your growth journey.

Key Takeaways:

- A growth mindset can transform not just individuals, but entire organizations.
- Embracing challenges and seeing effort as a path to mastery are key components of a growth mindset.
- Vulnerability plays a crucial role in adopting a true growth mindset.
- The discomfort that comes with growth is a sign of progress, not failure.
- A growth mindset has a ripple effect, influencing team culture and innovation.

As we wrap up this chapter, I want you to remember this: your mindset is not fixed. It's a choice you make every day, with every challenge you face, with every setback you encounter. Choosing a growth mindset doesn't mean choosing an easy path - often, it means choosing the harder path in the short term. But it's the path that leads to long-term success, fulfillment, and continuous improvement.

So, are you ready to embrace the growth mindset revolution? Are you prepared to see challenges as opportunities and effort as the path to mastery? The choice is yours. And I believe in you.

Let's rewire our brains for growth. Let's approach each day as an opportunity to learn and improve. Your next level of success is waiting on the other side of your next challenge. Go meet it with a growth mindset.

Chapter 6

Time Mastery - Harnessing Your Most Valuable Resource

> Time is the scarcest resource and unless it is managed nothing else can be managed."
> - Peter Drucker

In this chapter you will learn to master the art of time management through revolutionary strategies that transform how you approach your most precious and finite resource. Discover how successful entrepreneurs leverage time mastery techniques to achieve exponentially more while maintaining work-life balance and avoiding burnout. Learn practical frameworks to shift from being trapped by time to strategically investing it, maximizing both productivity and fulfillment in your entrepreneurial journey.

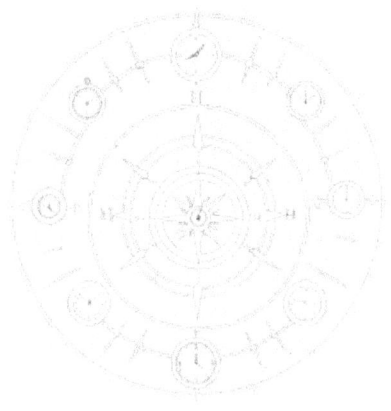

The alarm blared at 4:30 AM, jolting Elon Musk awake. As he rubbed the sleep from his eyes, his mind was already racing through the day ahead. Tesla, SpaceX, Neuralink, The Boring Company - how does one man juggle the demands of multiple groundbreaking companies? The answer lies not in superhuman abilities, but in a masterful approach to time management.

Musk's day is a carefully choreographed dance of productivity. He breaks his schedule into five-minute slots, a practice he calls "time boxing." Each moment is allocated with precision, from engineering meetings at SpaceX to production line walk-throughs at Tesla. But here's the kicker - Musk doesn't just manage his time; he bends it to his will.

This chapter isn't just about Musk's time management. It's about you - the aspiring entrepreneur, the visionary, the hustler. It's about transforming your relationship with time from a constant battle into a powerful alliance. Are you ready to master the art of time and catapult your entrepreneurial journey to new heights? Let's dive in.

Psychology of Time Perception: Time Is Not a Currency You Spend, But an Investment You Make

Before we delve into techniques, let's understand how our brains perceive time. Dr. Philip Zimbardo, renowned psychologist and author of "The Time Paradox," argues that our perception of time profoundly influences our decisions and actions.

Research shows that entrepreneurs with a future-oriented time perspective are more likely to spot opportunities and take calculated risks. However, being too future-focused can lead to anxiety and burnout. The key is balance.

Action Step: Take the Zimbardo Time Perspective Inventory (ZTPI) online. Identify your dominant time perspective and reflect on how it impacts your entrepreneurial decisions.

Chapter 6: Time Mastery - Harnessing Your Most Valuable Resource

Time Warping: The Entrepreneur's Secret Weapon

Now, let's talk about a mind-bending concept: time warping. No, we're not talking about science fiction. We're talking about psychologically manipulating your perception of time to boost productivity.

Have you ever been so engrossed in a task that hours flew by like minutes? That's called a 'flow state,' and it's the holy grail of productivity. A study by McKinsey found that executives in flow states were five times more productive than their peers.

But here's the million-dollar question: How do you induce a flow state? The answer lies in a technique called 'deep work,' coined by Cal Newport. It involves focusing intensely on a cognitively demanding task without distraction.

Action Step: Implement a daily 'deep work' session. Start with 30 minutes and gradually increase to 2-3 hours. During this time, eliminate all distractions - no phone, no email, no social media. Watch your productivity soar.

The Eisenhower Matrix: Urgent vs. Important

Picture this: It's Monday morning. Your to-do list is a mile long. Emails are piling up. Your phone won't stop buzzing. Sound familiar? Welcome to the entrepreneur's dilemma.

Enter the Eisenhower Matrix, a powerful tool named after President Dwight D. Eisenhower. It categorizes tasks into four quadrants based on urgency and importance:

1. Urgent and Important: Do immediately
2. Important but Not Urgent: Schedule for later
3. Urgent but Not Important: Delegate
4. Neither Urgent nor Important: Eliminate

Here's the mind-blowing part: Most entrepreneurs spend too much time in quadrant 1, firefighting urgent issues. But the real game-changer is quadrant 2 - important tasks that aren't urgent. This is where strategic planning, relationship building, and personal development happen.

Action Step: For one week, categorize your tasks using the Eisenhower Matrix. Aim to spend at least 50% of your time on quadrant 2 activities. Track how this shifts your productivity and stress levels.

The Eisenhower Matrix

	URGENT	NOT URGENT
IMPORTANT	**DO** Crises Deadlines Problems	**SCHEDULE** Planning Prevention Relationship Building
NOT IMPORTANT	**DELEGATE** Interruptions Some Meetings Some Calls	**ELIMINATE** Time Wasters Pleasant Activities Some Mail

The Pomodoro Technique: Embracing the Power of Constraints

Let's get vulnerable for a moment. How many times have you sat down to work, only to find yourself doom-scrolling on social media an hour later? We've all been there. The culprit? Our brain's tendency to overestimate how long we can focus.

Enter the Pomodoro Technique, brainchild of Francesco Cirillo. The concept is simple yet powerful: Work in focused 25-minute sprints, followed by 5-minute breaks. After four "pomodoros," take a longer 15–30-minute break.

Why does this work? It leverages the psychology of constraints. By imposing a time limit, you create a sense of urgency that combats procrastination. Plus, the frequent breaks prevent mental fatigue and boost overall productivity.

Action Step: Download a Pomodoro timer app (like Forest or Focus To-Do). Use it for your next workday. Pay attention to how it affects your focus and output.

Time Blocking: The Elon Musk Method

Remember Elon Musk's five-minute slots? That's an extreme form of time blocking, a technique used by many successful entrepreneurs. The idea is to pre-allocate chunks of time for specific tasks or types of work.

Cal Newport, author of "Deep Work," swears by this method. He argues that time blocking forces you to confront the reality of how much time you actually have and how long tasks really take.

But here's the kicker - time blocking isn't about creating a rigid, inflexible schedule. It's about being intentional with your time while allowing for flexibility. Think of it as a roadmap for your day, not a set of unbreakable rules.

Action Step: Create a time-blocked schedule for tomorrow. Allocate time for deep work, meetings, email, and personal tasks. At the end of the day, reflect on what worked and what didn't. Iterate and improve.

The Surprising Link Between Time Management and Work-Life Balance

Now, let's address the elephant in the room – the one wearing a "hustle 24/7" t-shirt and bragging about pulling all-nighters. As entrepreneurs, we often wear our 80-hour workweeks like badges of honor. We post about the grind on social media, glorify sleeping in our offices, and somehow convince ourselves that exhaustion is a status symbol. I've been there, done that, and let me tell you – it's not just unsustainable, it's downright dangerous.

But here's a hard truth that might shake your whole perspective on "the grind": working longer hours doesn't necessarily mean higher productivity or success. In fact, the data suggests quite the opposite. A groundbreaking study by Stanford University found something that should make every workaholic entrepreneur pause, productivity per hour declines sharply when a person works more than 50 hours a week. After 55 hours, productivity drops so dramatically that putting in any more hours would be pointless. Let that sink in for a moment – those extra 30 hours you're so proud of? They might actually be making you less effective, not more.

Think about it like this: imagine trying to drive cross-country without ever stopping for gas, rest, or maintenance. Sure, you might cover a lot of ground initially, but eventually, your car's going to break down. Your body and mind work the same way. You can't continuously extract performance without investing in recovery.

But it's not just about productivity metrics. Poor work-life balance creates a cascade of negative effects that many entrepreneurs don't see until it's too late. I learned this lesson the hard way early in my entrepreneurial journey. I was running multiple businesses, barely sleeping, missing my kids' important moments, and telling myself it was all worth it for the "greater good" of building my empire. My relationships were strained, my health was deteriorating, and ironically, my decision-making – the very thing my businesses needed most – was becoming increasingly poor due to exhaustion.

Here's a personal story for you., I remember sitting in my home office one night at 11 PM after a long day at work, staring at financials that had become blurry from fatigue, when it hit me: I wasn't working these insane hours because the work actually required it. I was doing it because I thought that's what successful entrepreneurs were supposed to do. I had bought into the myth that sacrifice, and suffering were prerequisites for success.

So, how do we strike a balance? It starts with fundamentally reframing how we view time. Instead of seeing it as a resource to be maximized, squeezed, and exploited until there's nothing left, we need to view it as a tool for holistic life satisfaction. This isn't about working less – it's about working smarter not harder and living fuller.

Think of your time like an investment portfolio. Just as you wouldn't put all your money into a single stock, you shouldn't invest all your time into work alone. You need to diversify. Sometime needs to go into your business, yes, but you also need to invest in your health, your relationships, your personal growth, and your mental wellbeing. These aren't indulgences – they're essential investments that pay dividends in every area of your life, including your business.

This means scheduling your workout with the same commitment as your board meeting. It means treating date night with your spouse as seriously as a client presentation. It means understanding that time spent playing with your kids or grandkids isn't time "away" from your business – its time investing in the very things that give your work meaning and purpose.

When you start viewing time through this lens, something remarkable happens. You become more intentional with how you spend it. You start questioning those long hours, not because you're lazy, but because you're strategic. You begin to focus on output rather than input, on impact rather than activity.

The most successful entrepreneurs I know aren't the ones working the longest hours – they're the ones who've mastered the art of time allocation. They understand that true productivity isn't about quantity of hours, but quality of focus. They've learned that the key to sustainable success isn't working themselves to exhaustion but maintaining the balance that allows them to bring their best selves to everything they do.

Action Step: Conduct a "time audit" for one week. Track how you spend every hour, including work, leisure, and sleep. Identify areas where you're overworking and underinvesting in your personal life. Make a plan to rebalance.

The 2-Minute Rule: Small Actions, Big Impact

Let's end with a simple yet powerful technique that can revolutionize your productivity: the 2-minute rule. Coined by David Allen in his book "Getting Things Done," it states: If a task will take less than two minutes, do it immediately. This rule combats procrastination and prevents small tasks from piling up into overwhelming mountains. But it's true power lies in building momentum. Each completed task, no matter how small, gives you a hit of dopamine, motivating you to tackle bigger challenges

Action Step:

For the next week, implement the 2-minute rule. If a task will take less than 2 minutes, do it immediately. Keep a tally of how many small tasks you complete. Notice how this impacts your overall productivity and motivation.

Key Takeaways:

- Understand your time perspective and how it influences your decisions.
- Induce 'flow states' through deep work for maximum productivity.
- Use the Eisenhower Matrix to prioritize tasks effectively.
- Leverage the Pomodoro Technique to combat procrastination and maintain focus.
- Implement time blocking for intentional and flexible time management.
- Strive for work-life balance to prevent burnout and boost long-term success.
- Use the 2-minute rule to build momentum and prevent task buildup.

Remember, time management isn't about squeezing more tasks into your day. It's about making the most of your limited time to create a fulfilling, balanced life while achieving your entrepreneurial dreams.

As you implement these strategies, be kind to yourself. Time mastery is a skill, and like any skill, it takes practice. There will be days when you nail it, and days when you fall short. That's okay. What matters is that you keep showing up, keep iterating, and keep striving to make the most of this precious resource we call time. Now, go forth and conquer your day, one well-managed minute at a time. Your future self will thank you.

Chapter 7

The Network Effect - Building Relationships That Matter

> Your network is your net worth."
> - Porter Gale

In this chapter you'll discover how to build and nurture a powerful network that becomes your greatest asset in entrepreneurial success. Learn proven strategies for creating authentic connections that go beyond superficial networking to forge meaningful relationships that drive mutual growth and opportunity. Master the art of strategic relationship building while maintaining genuine authenticity, transforming your network from a list of contacts into a thriving ecosystem of support and collaboration.

Richard Branson stood on the tarmac, his wild hair whipping in the wind as he gazed at the gleaming Virgin Atlantic aircraft before him. It was 1984, and his fledgling airline was about to take its inaugural flight. But this moment wasn't just about planes and profits. It was a testament to the power of relationships.

You see, Branson didn't know the first thing about running an airline when he decided to take on British Airways. What he did have was an unparalleled ability to connect with people. From leasing that first Boeing 747 to securing landing slots at Gatwick Airport, every step of Virgin Atlantic's journey was paved by Branson's network.

As he watched the first passengers board, Branson couldn't help but smile. He knew that each handshake, each conversation, each relationship he'd cultivated over the years had led to this moment. Little did he know, this was just the beginning of an empire built on the foundation of strategic connections.

Now, I know what you're thinking. "Great story, Kay Kay, but I'm not Richard Branson. I don't have his charm or his resources." And you're right, you're not Branson. You're you. And that's your superpower. Because in the world of entrepreneurship, authenticity trumps charm every single time. I was also thinking the same way you are thinking, for several years before I dived into networking and realized the power of networking. Folks proximity is power.

Let's dive into the science of why networking matters so much. A study published in the Journal of Business Venturing found that entrepreneurs with larger, more diverse networks were 3.5 times more likely to achieve high growth in their ventures. Three and a half times! That's not just a nice-to-have, folks. That's the difference between scraping by and scaling up. You might have heard the Jim Rohn's saying "You are the average of the five people you spend the most time with."

But here's the kicker: it's not about having the biggest network. It's about having the right network. Quality over quantity, always. Dr. Ronald Burt, a sociologist at the University of Chicago, discovered something fascinating. He found that people who bridge "structural holes" - gaps between different groups in a network - have a significant advantage in generating good ideas and advancing their careers.

Think about it this way: if you only hang out with other entrepreneurs in your industry, you're all swimming in the same pool of ideas. But what if you connected with a doctor? Or an artist? Or hell, even a plumber? Suddenly, you're exposed to new perspectives, new problems, and new solutions. That's where the magic happens.

Now, let's talk about how you can start building these relationships that matter. I know what some of you are thinking – the very idea of networking makes your palms sweat. Walking into a room full of strangers and striking up conversations feels about as appealing as getting a root canal. Trust me, I get it. As an immigrant entrepreneur with a beard and a turban who started with very few connections in this country, I intimately understand how intimidating networking can feel. But I've learned that building meaningful relationships doesn't have to feel like a performance – in fact, it works better when it doesn't.

Start with Authenticity

Here's the game-changing truth I wish someone had told me years ago: forget everything you've learned about elevator pitches and polished presentations for a second. Stop rehearsing your "I'm a successful entrepreneur" speech in front of the mirror. Instead, focus on something much more powerful: being human. Share your passions – even the ones that have nothing to do with business. You'd be amazed how many doors open when you drop the professional facade and show your true colors.

I remember being at a laundromat conference for the first time, feeling completely out of place among the industry veterans. But when I mentioned my passion for using artificial intelligence in entrepreneurship, suddenly the conversation shifted. A senior executive with a reputed company started sharing stories about his own passion in artificial intelligence and how they use it in their business, and that authentic connection led to a connection that has been invaluable for both our businesses.

Action Step: Before your next networking event, write down three unique things about yourself that have nothing to do with your business. Maybe it's your love of 80s movies, your weekend hiking adventures, or your quest to find the perfect biryani recipe. Use these as conversation starters. They're not just ice breakers – they're authenticity builders.

Listen More Than You Speak

Here's a networking superpower that too few people utilize: strategic listening. Everyone loves to talk about themselves. So let them. But – and this is crucial – don't just wait for your turn to speak. Listen with genuine curiosity. Ask thoughtful follow-up questions. Show real interest in understanding their journey, their challenges, their victories.

Think about it like this: when you're truly listening, you're not just being polite – you're gathering intelligence. Every conversation is an opportunity to learn something new, gain a different perspective, or identify ways you might be able to help later.

Exercise: Practice the 2:1 ratio. For every statement you make about yourself, ask two questions about the other person. But not just any questions – ask ones that dig deeper than surface-level small talk. Instead of "What do you do?" try "What made you choose this industry?" or "What's the most exciting project you're working on right now?"

Give Before You Take

This is where so many people get networking backwards. They go into every interaction thinking, "What can I get out of this?" Instead, flip the script. Make your first thought, "How can I add value to this person's life or business?"

Networking isn't about collecting business cards or adding LinkedIn connections. It's about building a community of mutual support and growth. Always be the first to start the conversation and be on the lookout for ways to help others, whether it's making an introduction, sharing a relevant article, offering your expertise, or even just providing a different perspective on a challenge they're facing.

I've made it a habit to keep a "connection journal" where I note down people's interests, challenges, and goals. This allows me to make meaningful introductions when opportunities arise. Just last month, I was able to connect two people from different networking events who ended up forming a successful partnership in a multifamily property– all because I listened to what they were exactly looking for.

Challenge: For the next week, reach out to one person in your network each day with an offer to help, no strings attached. Maybe you saw an article that made you think of them, or you know someone they should meet, or you have experience with a challenge they're facing. The key is to expect nothing in return.

Embrace Digital Platforms (Don't Hide Behind Them)

In today's digital age, social media platforms like LinkedIn, Twitter, Facebook, and Instagram are invaluable networking tools. They're great for making initial connections and staying visible in your network. But here's the crucial part – don't let your networking stop at likes and comments.

Use these platforms as launching pads for real conversations. When you have an interesting exchange in the comments, take it to DMs. When you've built some rapport in DMs, suggest a telephone or a video call. When you've had a few good video calls, look for opportunities to meet in person if possible.

The real magic of networking happens in real conversations, whether they're through telephone calls, video chats, or face-to-face meetings. That's where you can build genuine rapport, share deeper insights, and create lasting connections. Do not forget to have a digital business card on your phone to exchange.

Action Step: Identify three online like-minded connections you'd like to know better. Reach out and invite them for a virtual coffee chat and even a cup of coffee at Starbucks if that is possible. Make sure to follow-up with them after the meeting.

Diversify Your Network

Remember those structural holes we talked about? They're the gaps between different social and professional circles, and they're potential gold mines for innovative ideas and unexpected opportunities. Think about it – if you're only networking with people in your exact industry, with similar backgrounds and experiences, you're essentially swimming in the same pool. The real magic happens when you start building bridges across different worlds.

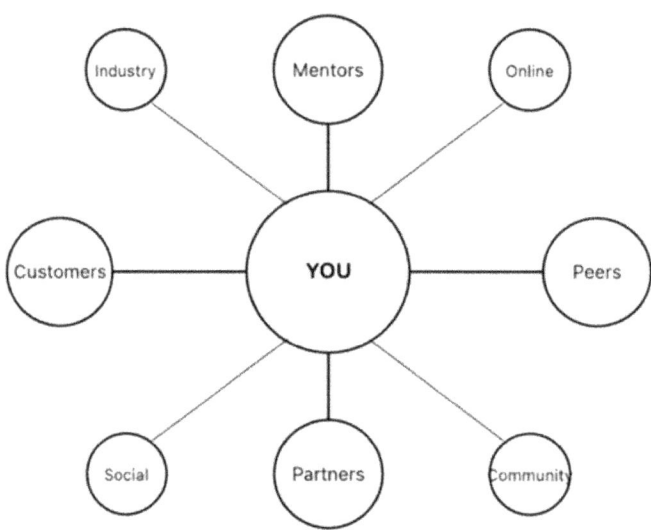

Chapter 7: The Network Effect - Building Relationships That Matter

Exercise: Create a network map. Draw circles representing different areas of your life (work, hobbies, skills, interests or community, etc.). Identify areas where you have few connections and plan to expand in those directions.

Now, let's get real for a second. Building meaningful relationships takes time, effort, and yes, vulnerability. It means putting yourself out there, risking rejection, and sometimes feeling like a total impostor. But here's the truth: everyone feels that way sometimes.

In his autobiography, Branson admits, "I have always suffered from what others might call 'shyness' and what I call extreme reserve... I still have to psych myself up for public speaking." See? Even the masters of networking have their moments of doubt. The key is to push through that discomfort. Because on the other side of that awkward small talk, that stuttered introduction, that fear of looking foolish, lies the potential for connections that could change your life and your business.

Here's a personal story for you. When I first ventured into real estate investing, approaching potential investors felt like scaling a mountain without gear. Despite my thorough market research and promising property analysis, self-doubt crept in. Here I was, an immigrant entrepreneur with a successful Gas Station & convenience stores and Laundromats business background, trying to convince investors to trust me with multimillion-dollar apartment deals. The fear of rejection was paralyzing, and the responsibility of managing others' wealth felt overwhelming. But I realized that my Gas Station & convenience stores success story, immigrant work ethic, helpful nature, honesty and commitment to transparent business practices weren't weaknesses—they were my unique value proposition.

So, I started small. I reached out to family and friends and fellow entrepreneurs in my local community. To my surprise, most were happy to chat, no doubt there were some rejections. As my confidence grew, I aimed higher. I remember the day I landed at an interview with a world-famous surgeon who met me on social media. My hands were shaking as I dialed his number. But you know what? It turned out to be one of the best conversations of my life because by then I was one of the best in my field and had a lot of knowledge about my industry. That interview led to more high-profile investors by his referral, which led to more and more investors, I never could have imagined. All because I was willing to push past my limited belief, self-doubt, fear and had the courage to make that call.

Now, I want you to think about your own network. Who are the people who inspire you, challenge you, support you? Who are the ones you turn to when you need advice or a reality check? These are your ride-or-dies, your personal board of directors. Treasure them. Nurture those relationships. But also think about the gaps in your network. Where could you use more diverse perspectives? What skills or knowledge are you missing? These are your growth opportunities.

Here's an exercise to help you map out your network and identify areas for growth:

1. Grab a piece of paper and draw a circle in the center. This is you. Open the contacts list on your phone.
2. Around that circle, draw five to seven smaller circles. Label each with a different area of your life or business (e.g., industry peers, mentors, potential clients, personal growth, entrepreneurs etc.).
3. In each circle, write the names of people who fit that category in your network.
4. Now, look at your map. Where are the circles fullest? Where are they sparse?
5. For the areas that need growth, brainstorm three specific actions you can take to expand your network in that direction.

Remember, building a strong network isn't about collecting business cards or racking up LinkedIn connections. It's about fostering and nurturing genuine relationships with people who challenge you, support you, and help you grow. It's about creating a community of like-minded individuals who are all pushing each other to be better.

So, here's my challenge to you: In the next 30 days, commit to strengthening your network. Reach out to one new person each week. Reconnect with someone you've lost touch with. Offer help or value to someone in your network without expecting anything in return. Even try to get on a video call which is very powerful and make sure to follow-up.

Will it be comfortable? Not always. Will there be moments of awkwardness? Probably. But remember why you're doing this. Remember the doors that can open, the opportunities that can arise, the growth that can happen when you connect with the right people. You have the power to build a network that can transform your business and your life. You have the ability to create connections that lift you up, challenge you to grow, and open doors you never even knew existed.

So, are you ready to grow your network? Are you ready to build relationships that truly matter? The choice is yours. Proximity is Power. And I believe in you.

Let's get connecting. Let's start building those bridges. Your next big opportunity, your next game-changing insight, your next powerful ally - they're all waiting for you in your network. Go find them.

Action Steps:

1. Conduct a network audit using the mapping exercise.
2. Set a goal to reach out to one new person and reconnect with one existing contact each week for the next month.
3. Before your next networking event, prepare three unique facts about yourself to use as conversation starters.
4. Practice the 2:1 listening ratio in your next three conversations.
5. Identify one area where your network is lacking and make a specific plan to expand in that direction.

Key Takeaways:

- Quality trumps quantity in networking. Focus on building meaningful relationships, not just collecting contacts and keep the connections alive.
- Diversity in your network leads to more innovative ideas and opportunities.
- Authenticity and vulnerability are key to forming genuine connections.
- Giving value to others is the fastest way to grow your network.
- Networking is a skill that can be developed with practice and persistence.

Remember, your network is your net worth. But more than that, it's your support system, your brain trust, your ladder to growth. Nurture it. Expand it. And watch as it transforms not just your business, but your entire entrepreneurial journey.

Chapter 8

Financial Intelligence - The Language of Business Success

> The most important investment you can make is in yourself."
> - Warren Buffett

In this chapter you will learn to master the critical financial language of business success by developing deep financial intelligence that transforms numbers into strategic insights. Learn how successful entrepreneurs leverage financial understanding to make better decisions, spot opportunities, and build sustainable wealth through their ventures. Discover practical frameworks that make financial mastery accessible and actionable, moving beyond basic accounting to true financial leadership.

Ray Kroc stood in the bustling kitchen of the first McDonald's restaurant in San Bernardino, California, mesmerized by the efficiency of the operation. It was 1954, and Kroc, a 52-year-old milkshake mixer salesman, had just stumbled upon what he believed was a gold mine. But it wasn't just the speedy service or the quality of the food that caught his eye. It was the numbers.

As he watched the McDonald brothers ring up sale after sale, Kroc's mind was already racing, calculating potential profits, expansion costs, and economies of scale. You see, Kroc wasn't just a salesman; he was a financial visionary. He understood that the true language of business success wasn't just about flipping burgers—it was about mastering the numbers. Fast forward to today, and McDonald's is a global empire worth billion dollars, all because one man saw beyond the grill and into the ledger. This, my friends, is the power of financial intelligence.

Now, I know what some of you are thinking. "Kay Kay, I'm not a numbers person. I got into business to follow my passion, not to crunch numbers." And believe me, I get it. When I first started out, the mere thought of financial statements made my eyes glaze over. But here's the truth bomb I'm about to drop on you: if you want your business to thrive, you need to get comfortable with the financial side of things. It's not just about making money—it's about understanding it, growing it, and using it as a tool to build something sustainable.

Let's break down why financial intelligence is so crucial for entrepreneurs. Think of financial intelligence as your business's GPS system—without it, you're essentially driving blindfolded through the complex terrain of entrepreneurship.

1. It Helps You Make Informed Decisions When you understand your finances, you're no longer shooting in the dark. Every decision, from pricing strategies to hiring new talent to expansion opportunities, becomes grounded in solid financial reality rather than gut feelings or assumptions. A comprehensive study by the Financial Industry Regulatory Authority revealed something fascinating: individuals with higher financial literacy were not just marginally better at making financial decisions—

Chapter 8: Financial Intelligence - The Language of Business Success

they were significantly more likely to engage in behaviors that boosted their bottom line and created sustainable growth.

Try this: Set aside a "Financial Power Hour" each week. Find a quiet time when you're mentally fresh. During this hour, dive deep into your balance sheets, financial statements and KPIs. Don't just skim the surface—analyze trends, identify patterns, and look for both red flags and golden opportunities. Ask yourself: "What story are these numbers telling me about my business?"

2. It Reduces Stress Let's get real for a moment. Money worries keep entrepreneurs up at night—How do I know because I've been there. The American Psychological Association's research isn't just statistics; it's a reflection of a very real challenge we face as business owners. But here's the beautiful thing: when you develop financial intelligence, you transform that anxiety into confidence. Those with higher financial literacy reported significantly lower stress levels, not because they had more money, but because they understood and could control their financial situation better.

Challenge yourself: Create what I call a "Financial Control Center"—a detailed budget that tracks every dollar entering and leaving your business for the next 30 days. Break it down into categories that make sense for your business, may be Income and Expense category. Don't just track the numbers; understand the story behind each transaction. Why did that expense increase? Why did that revenue stream decrease? Knowledge is power, and in this case, it's also peace of mind.

3. It Attracts Investors and Partners: In the world of business, numbers are the universal language. When you can speak this language fluently, you open doors to opportunities that might otherwise remain closed. CB Insights' research revealed a sobering truth: running out of cash isn't just a minor setback—it's often a business killer, second only to building products nobody wants. This isn't just about having money; it's about understanding and communicating your financial story effectively.

Make it a habit: Practice what I call the "Investor Pitch Mirror Exercise." Stand in front of a mirror and explain your business finances in clear, compelling terms. Break down complex financial concepts into simple, relatable stories. Remember, great financial communication isn't about showing how much you know—it's about helping others understand your business's financial journey and potential.

4. It Helps You Plan for the Future: Financial intelligence is your business's crystal ball. The Journal of Business Venturing's study didn't just find a causal link between financial literacy and planning—it found that entrepreneurs who truly understood their finances were substantially more likely to engage in effective long-term budgeting, planning and, crucially, achieved better business outcomes.

Practice this: Create a "Financial Vision Map." Set clear, specific financial goals for your business across three-time horizons: one year (tactical), three years (strategic), and five years (visionary). For each goal, outline the specific financial metrics you'll track and the key milestones you'll need to hit. Remember, a goal without a plan is just a wish.

5. It Protects You in Tough Times: Every business faces storms—that's just the nature of entrepreneurship. The U.S. Small Business Administration's findings confirm what successful entrepreneurs have known for years: strong financial management isn't just about growing in good times; it's about surviving and even thriving in challenging times. Think of it as building your business's financial immune system.

Start small: Begin building what I call your "Business Security Shield"—an emergency fund that can cover 3-6 months of expenses. This isn't just about saving money; it's about creating peace of mind and strategic flexibility. Start with small, consistent contributions to this saving account and watch your security shield grow stronger month by month.

Remember, financial intelligence isn't just about numbers—it's about empowerment. It's about transforming your relationship with money from one of anxiety and uncertainty to one of confidence and control. When you truly understand your finances, you're not just running a business; you're masterfully conducting a financial symphony.

Now, I can hear some of you saying, "But Kay Kay, I'm just not good with numbers. This stuff doesn't come naturally to me." And you know what? That's okay. Financial intelligence isn't about being a math whiz. It's about understanding the basics and being willing to learn. It is a skill and can be learned.

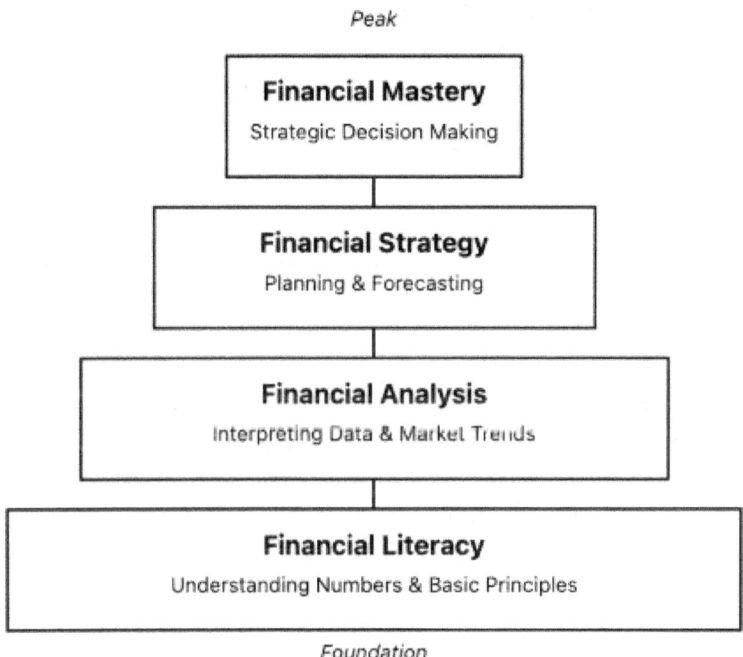

So how do you actually build your financial intelligence? Here are some strategies that have worked for me and many other successful entrepreneurs:

1. Educate Yourself: There are tons of great books, courses, and podcasts on financial management for entrepreneurs. Commit to continuous learning. Warren Buffett, one of the most successful investors of all time, spends 80% of his working day reading and thinking.

2. Use Technology: Take advantage of accounting software and apps that can make financial management easier and more automated. A study by Xero found that small businesses that use cloud accounting software get paid 33% faster than those who don't.

3. Understand Your Cash Flow: Cash is the lifeblood of your business. Know exactly how much is coming in and going out, at all times. A study by U.S. Bank found that 82% of business failures are due to poor cash management.

4. Keep Personal and Business Finances Separate: This is crucial for legal and tax reasons, and it makes it much easier to track your business finances. A survey by Clutch found that 27% of small business owners don't have a separate bank account for their business.

5. Plan for Taxes: Don't let tax season catch you off guard. Set aside money for taxes throughout the year. The IRS estimates that 40% of small businesses incur an average penalty of $845 per year for late or incorrect filings.

Remember, becoming financially intelligent is a journey, not a destination. It's about continuous learning and improvement.

Here's a powerful truth I want you to internalize: Your level of financial intelligence will often determine the ceiling of your success. You can be the best in the world at what you do, but if you can't manage the money side of things, your business will always struggle.

So, I challenge you: For the next 30 days, commit to improving your financial intelligence. Spend at least 15 minutes each day learning about a financial concept. Start tracking your business finances more closely. Have conversations about money—with your accountant, with team, with mentors, with other entrepreneurs. Will it be comfortable? Not always, especially if you're not used to focusing on finances. Will there be a learning curve? Absolutely. But remember why you're doing this. Remember the clarity, the confidence, and the control that come with true financial intelligence.

Chapter 8: Financial Intelligence - The Language of Business Success

Action Step: Create a Financial Dashboard

To put this into practice right away, I want you to create a financial dashboard for your business (or future business if you're just starting out). This dashboard should give you a quick, visual overview of your key financial metrics. Here's how to do it:

1. Identify Your Key Performance Indicators (KPIs): These might include revenue, profit margin, cash flow, customer acquisition cost, and lifetime customer value.
2. Choose a Tool: This could be as simple as a spreadsheet or as sophisticated as a business intelligence platform like QuickBooks.
3. Gather Your Data: Pull the necessary numbers from your accounting software, sales reports, and other relevant sources.
4. Design Your Dashboard: Create visual representations of your KPIs using charts and graphs.
5. Set Up Regular Updates: Decide how often you'll update your dashboard (weekly, monthly, quarterly) and stick to it.

Remember, what gets measured gets managed. By creating this dashboard, you're taking a huge step towards greater financial intelligence and control of your business.

Now, let's address the elephant in the room. I know some of you are thinking, "Kay Kay, this all sounds great, but I'm an entrepreneur because I want to create, to innovate. I don't want to be bogged down by numbers." I get it. I really do. But here's the thing: financial intelligence isn't just about bean counting. It's about creative problem-solving.

Think about it this way: Every number on your financial statement tells a story. Your revenue? That's the story of how well you're connecting with your customers. Your expenses? They tell the tale of how efficiently you're running your operation. Your profit margin, the bottom line? That's the narrative of how well you're balancing value creation with cost management. When you start to see finances this way, it becomes a creative exercise. It's about crafting the story of your business, chapter by chapter, quarter by quarter.

Let me share a personal story. When I first expanded my gas station business, my hands-on management style became my blind spot. I prided myself on keeping the stations spotlessly clean, equipment running smoothly, and customers happy. But beneath this polished operation, our financials were bleeding. I was investing heavily in equipment, assuming customer satisfaction automatically meant profitability but not focusing on ROI. It wasn't until I deep dived into our books that I discovered we were barely breaking even despite its busy appearance. This wake-up call transformed how I approached business—teaching me that success lies not just in operational excellence, but in understanding the story my finances were telling me.

So, I challenge you to reframe how you think about financial intelligence. It's not a chore—it's a superpower. It's the ability to see the hidden patterns in your business, to spot opportunities others miss, and to make decisions based on insight rather than instinct. As you embark on this journey of financial intelligence, remember it's not about becoming an accountant. It's about becoming a more well-rounded, insightful, and effective entrepreneur so that you could make well informed business decisions. It's about giving yourself the tools to turn your vision into reality.

You have the power to master your business finances. You have the ability to make smart, informed decisions that will drive your business forward. And in doing so, you'll not only build a more successful business—you'll build a more secure, stable future for yourself and those who depend on you.

So, are you ready to level up your financial game? Are you ready to speak the language of business success fluently? The choice is yours. And I believe in you.

Let's crunch those numbers. Let's make those dollars work for you. Your next level of success is waiting on the other side of financial mastery. Go seize it.

Key Takeaways:

- Financial intelligence is crucial for making informed business decisions.
- Understanding your finances reduces stress and attracts investors.
- Strong financial management helps businesses survive tough times.
- Financial literacy is a skill that can be learned and improved over time.
- Viewing finances as a storytelling tool can make it a more engaging and creative process.

Remember, the greatest investment you can make is in yourself. By developing your financial intelligence, you're not just improving your business—you're investing in your own growth as an entrepreneur. Now go forth and conquer those numbers!

Chapter 9

Innovation Ignition - Sparking Creativity in Your Venture

> Innovation distinguishes between a leader and a follower."
> - Steve Jobs

In this chapter you'll discover how to ignite and sustain innovation in your business by mastering the art of creative problem-solving and breakthrough thinking. Learn proven techniques for fostering a culture of innovation that transforms challenges into opportunities and conventional thinking into revolutionary solutions. Master practical strategies for making innovation a consistent, reliable force in your venture rather than just occasional moments of inspiration.

James Dyson stood in his workshop, surrounded by 5,126 failed prototypes. Most people would have given up long ago, but Dyson wasn't most people. He was an entrepreneur with a vision – to create a vacuum cleaner that never lost suction. As he stared at the latest failed attempt, a thought struck him: "What if I make it bigger?"

This seemingly simple idea led to the creation of the world's first bagless vacuum cleaner, revolutionizing an industry that hadn't seen significant innovation in decades. Dyson's story isn't just about perseverance (though there's plenty of that). It's about the power of innovative thinking in entrepreneurship.

But here's the kicker: Dyson's breakthrough didn't come from some magical burst of genius. It came from years of tinkering, failing, and most importantly, thinking differently about a common problem. And that, my fellow entrepreneurs, is the essence of innovation.

The Psychology of Creativity: It's Not Just for "Creatives"

Now, I know what some of you are thinking. "Kay Kay, I'm not the creative type. I'm more of a numbers person." Well, I've got news for you: creativity isn't some mystical gift bestowed upon a chosen few. It's a skill, and like any other skill, it can be developed and learned.

Dr. Carol Dweck's research on mindset offers some fascinating insights here. She found that people with a "growth mindset" – those who believe their abilities can be developed through dedication and hard work – are more likely to embrace challenges and persist in the face of setbacks. Sound familiar? It should, because that's exactly what successful entrepreneurs do.

But here's where it gets really interesting. A study published in the Journal of Business Venturing found that entrepreneurs with a growth mindset were more likely to engage in innovative behaviors and, consequently, achieve greater success in their ventures. In other words, believing in your ability to be creative actually makes you more creative.

Chapter 9: Innovation Ignition - Sparking Creativity in Your Venture

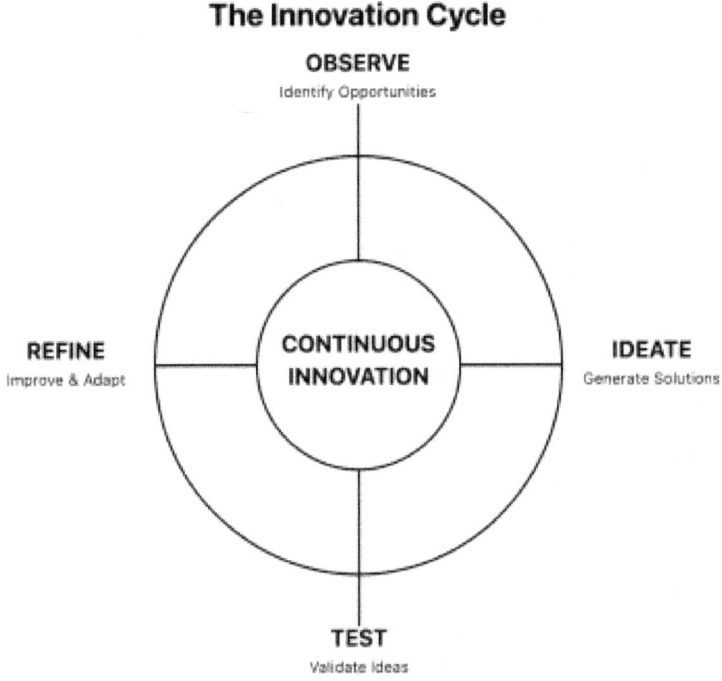

So, let's bust this myth once and for all: You don't need to be a "creative genius" to innovate. You just need to be willing to think differently and persist through failures.

Igniting Innovation: Practical Techniques for Your Business

Alright, so now that we've established that you can be innovative (yes, you!), let's talk about how to actually do it. Innovation isn't some mystical force that strikes like lightning—it's a skill that can be developed and sharpened through specific practices. Here are some powerful techniques that have worked for me and countless other entrepreneurs:

1.Embrace Constraints: Remember how Dyson's breakthrough came when he decided to make the vacuum bigger? Sometimes, limitations can spark creativity. I learned this lesson firsthand in my laundromat business. When faced with limited square footage, instead of seeing it as a handicap, we turned it into an advantage by optimizing our layout and replacing with large washers and increasing the total washer capacity so effectively that our revenue per square foot exceeded industry averages.

Try this: List your top three business constraints right now. For each one, ask yourself: "How could this limitation actually be an advantage?" You might be surprised at how restrictions can spark innovative solutions.

2.Cross-Pollinate Ideas: Some of the most innovative ideas come from combining concepts from different fields. Airbnb, for instance, applied the sharing economy concept to hospitality, creating a whole new business model. Think about Netflix—they combined movie rentals with postal delivery, then with streaming technology, and finally with content creation. Each combination created a new innovation.

Challenge yourself: Spend 30 minutes each week exploring an industry completely different from yours. What ideas or approaches could you adapt for your business? For example, what could a restaurant learn from a car manufacturer about efficiency? What could a tech company learn from a yoga studio about customer experience?

3.Question Everything: Challenge assumptions about your industry. Why are things done a certain way? Could there be a better approach? This isn't about being contrarian—it's about being curious. When I started in Single family real estate property management, I questioned the traditional approach of doing all property tours in person. By implementing virtual tours early on, we were able to attract out-of-city and state tenants more efficiently than our competitors.

Practice this: Create an "Assumption Log" for your industry. List all the "that's just how it's done" practices. Then, for each one, ask: "What if we did the opposite? What if we eliminated this step entirely? What if we combined this with something else?"

4.Encourage Diverse Perspectives: Surround yourself with people who think differently from you. Diversity isn't just about demographics—it's about diversity of thought. Studies show that diverse teams are 45% more likely to improve market share and 70%

more likely to capture new markets. But here's the key: you need to actively create an environment where different perspectives are not just heard but valued.

Make it happen: Create an "Innovation Circle" with people from different industries, backgrounds, and thinking styles. Meet regularly to discuss challenges and brainstorm solutions. The only rule? No idea is too crazy to consider.

5. Make Time for Creativity: Innovation doesn't happen in the margins. You can't expect breakthrough ideas to emerge while you're rushing between meetings or answering emails. You need to schedule dedicated time for ideation and creative thinking. Think of it as your "Innovation Power Hour."

Structure it like this: Set aside at least one hour each week purely for creative thinking. No emails, no phone calls, no interruptions.

Use this time to:

- Review your Assumption Log
- Explore cross-industry ideas
- Sketch out "what if" scenarios
- Map potential innovations

Remember, this isn't "free time" or "wasted time"—it's strategic innovation time. Just as you wouldn't skip a crucial business meeting, don't skip your innovation sessions. But here's the crucial part: innovation isn't just about having ideas—it's about implementing them. For each innovative idea you decide to pursue, create what I call an "Innovation Action Plan":

- Clearly define the innovation
- Identify potential obstacles
- List required resources
- Set specific milestones
- Establish success metrics
- Create a timeline for implementation

Start small if you need to. Test your innovations in controlled environments before rolling them out broadly. Remember, even small innovations can lead to significant improvements over time.

The key is to make innovation a habit, not an event. By consistently applying these techniques and making time for creative thinking, you'll develop an innovation mindset that becomes second nature. As Thomas Edison said, "Innovation is 1% inspiration and 99% perspiration." So, get ready to put in the work—your next breakthrough idea awaits.

Your innovation journey starts now. Which of these techniques will you implement first? The choice is yours, but whatever you choose, commit to it fully. Remember, in today's fast-paced business world, the ability to innovate isn't just nice to have—it's essential for survival and success.

The Unexpected Connection: Constraints and Creativity

Now, here's something that might blow your mind: constraints can actually boost creativity. I know, it sounds counterintuitive. But hear me out.

A study published in the Journal of Consumer Research found that people generate more creative ideas when they're given limitations. It's like what Dr. Seuss did when he wrote "Green Eggs and Ham" using only 50 unique words on a bet. The constraint forced him to be more creative, resulting in one of the best-selling children's books of all time.

In the business world, we see this principle at work in companies like IKEA. Their constraint? Flat-pack furniture that customers assemble themselves. This limitation led to innovative designs, lower costs, and a unique brand identity that's recognizable worldwide. So, the next time you're faced with a constraint in your business, don't curse it. Embrace it. It might just be the key to your next big innovation.

Exercise: The "Worst Possible Idea" Technique

Alright, it's time to put this into practice. We're going to use a technique called the "Worst Possible Idea." Here's how it works:

1. Think of a current challenge in your business.
2. Now, brainstorm the absolute worst, most ridiculous solutions to this problem. The more outlandish, the better.
3. Look at each bad idea and ask, "What makes this so terrible?"
4. Now, flip it. How could you turn this bad idea into a good one?

This technique works because it takes the pressure off coming up with a "brilliant" idea right away. It allows you to think more freely and often leads to unexpected insights.

For example, let's say your challenge is increasing customer engagement. A "worst" idea might be to spam your customers with constant emails and texts. That's terrible because it's annoying and would likely drive customers away. But flip it: What if you created a system where customers could customize exactly what kind of notifications they receive and when? Suddenly, you've got an idea for a personalized communication system that could significantly boost engagement.

Vulnerability: The Secret Ingredient of Innovative Leadership

Now, let's talk about something that doesn't get discussed enough in entrepreneurship: vulnerability. Brené Brown's research as I have talked before has shown that vulnerability – the willingness to take risks and expose ourselves to uncertainty – is crucial for innovation and creativity.

As entrepreneurs, we often feel pressure to have all the answers. But here's the truth: admitting when you don't know something or when you've failed can actually make you a stronger, more innovative and creative leader.

I'll share a personal story. In 2012, when I ventured into the laundromat business, I faced a pivotal decision. My equipment distributor recommended implementing a card-only payment system—a radical departure from the traditional coin-operated model that had defined the industry for decades. The term "coin laundromat" was so ingrained in the public consciousness that there were no card-only establishments in the market at the time.

Drawing on my technology background, I could envision the transformative potential of a card operated laundromat. Despite the inherent risks of being an early adopter, I took the leap and launched a card-only facility. This innovative approach enabled us to implement sophisticated loyalty programs and customer engagement features that would have been impossible with traditional coin operations. That made us totally different from our competitors. The market validated our forward-thinking strategy, and today we proudly operate four successful card-operated laundromats, proving that embracing technological advancement was the right choice for our business.

The Approach to Innovation: Where Possibility Meets Purpose, Progress Takes Flight

Alright, let's cut the crap. Here's the hard truth about innovation: it's not always about coming up with something totally new. Sometimes, it's about taking something that already exists and making it better or applying it in a new way. Take Uber, for example. They didn't invent taxis or smartphones or GPS. They just combined these existing elements in a new way that solved a common problem. That's innovation, folks.

So, stop putting so much pressure on yourself to come up with the "next big thing." Instead, focus on solving problems. Look at what's frustrating you or your customers and think about how you could make it better. And here's another truth bomb: not every idea needs to be revolutionary. Small, incremental innovations can add up to big changes over time. It's like compound interest for your business.

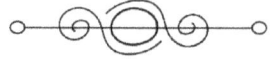

Action Steps:

1. Mindset Shift: Take the Mindset Quiz online to identify areas where you might have a fixed mindset about creativity and innovation. Choose one area to focus on shifting to a growth mindset this week.

2. Innovation Habit: Set aside 30 minutes each day for the next week to engage in a creative activity unrelated to your business. This could be drawing, writing, or even solving puzzles. Pay attention to how this impacts your thinking in other areas.

3. Constraint Challenge: Choose a current business challenge. Now, add an arbitrary constraint (e.g., solve it using only resources you already have, or solve it in a way that also addresses an environmental issue). Brainstorm solutions within this constraint.

4. Vulnerability Practice: At your next team meeting, share a recent failure or uncertainty you've experienced. Encourage team members to do the same. Notice how this impacts the group dynamic and the ideas that emerge.

5. Problem-Solving Focus: Identify three pain points your customers regularly experience. For each one, brainstorm at least five potential solutions, no matter how wild they seem. Remember, bad ideas can lead to good ones!

Key Takeaways:

- Innovation isn't about being a "creative genius" – it's a skill that can be developed.
- Constraints can actually boost creativity by forcing you to think differently.
- Diversity of thought is crucial for fostering innovation in your business.

- Vulnerability and admitting what you don't know can lead to more authentic and innovative leadership.
- Innovation doesn't always mean inventing something new – it can be about combining existing elements in new ways or making incremental improvements.

Remember, innovation isn't a one-time event. It's a mindset, a way of approaching problems and opportunities. By consistently applying these principles and techniques, you can create a culture of innovation in your business that will set you apart from the competition and drive your success.

Now go out there and innovate, you brilliant entrepreneur. The world is waiting for your ideas.

Chapter 10

The Confidence Equation - Building Unshakeable Self-Belief

> With realization of one's own potential and self-confidence in one's ability, one can build a better world."
> - Dalai Lama

In this chapter you'll learn how to unlock the power of authentic confidence and discover how to build unshakeable self-belief that transforms your entrepreneurial journey. Learn evidence-based strategies for developing genuine confidence that comes from competence and self-awareness, not bravado or external validation.

As the sun rose over the Mississippi town of Kosciusko, a young girl named Oprah Winfrey woke up in her grandmother's modest farmhouse. Born into poverty and faced with unimaginable adversity, Oprah had every reason to doubt herself. Yet, even at a young age, there was a spark in her eyes - a glimmer of self-belief that would one day transform her into one of the most influential media moguls in history.

Fast forward several decades, and that same spark had become a blazing fire. Oprah stood on stage, addressing millions of viewers worldwide, her confidence radiating through the screen. How did she transform from a girl born into poverty to a woman who could command the attention of the world? The answer lies in one powerful factor: confidence.

But here's the thing - Oprah's journey to confidence wasn't a straight line. It was filled with setbacks, moments of doubt, and periods of intense vulnerability. And that's precisely what made her confidence so potent. It wasn't a mask she put on; it was a force she cultivated from within.

Now, I can hear some of you thinking, "That's great for Oprah, Kay Kay, but I'm not a natural-born confident person." And you know what? That's okay. Because here's the truth bomb, I'm about to drop on you: confidence isn't something you're born with - it's something you build over time like any other skill..

The Science of Self-Confidence: Transform Self-Doubt into Data-Driven Growth

Let's geek out for a moment and look at what science tells us about confidence. A study published in the Journal of Personality and Social Psychology found that self-confidence was a stronger predictor of success than actual ability. In other words, believing in yourself can sometimes be more important than your skills or resources.

But it gets even more interesting. Neuroscientists have found that when we feel confident, our brains release a cocktail of chemicals - dopamine, serotonin, and oxytocin - that not only make us feel good but also enhance our performance. It's like a biological superpower that we can activate at will.

So, why is confidence so crucial for entrepreneurs? Let us break it down.

Let me tell you, it's not just about feeling good—it's about creating tangible results in your business. Let's break this down into five game-changing ways confidence transforms your entrepreneurial journey:

1. It Fuels Risk-Taking: When you're confident and knowledgeable, you're more willing to take calculated risks. And in entrepreneurship, calculated risks are often the steppingstones to success. Think about Sara Blakely, who invested her life savings of $5,000 to start Spanx. She wasn't reckless—she was confident in her product and her ability to make it succeed.

Try this: Write down one bold move you've been hesitating to make in your business. Now, imagine yourself taking that step with complete confidence. How does it feel? Don't just think about it—really feel it in your body. What changes in your posture? Your breathing? Your energy? Now, break that bold move into smaller, actionable steps. Remember, confidence isn't about blind leaps—it's about trust in your preparation and ability to handle whatever comes.

2. It Attracts Opportunities: Confidence is magnetic. It draws people and opportunities to you like a moth to a flame. I've seen this countless times in my own journey. When I started speaking about multifamily investing with genuine confidence—not arrogance, but authentic belief in my knowledge and experience— the quality of my networking conversations transformed. People weren't just listening; they were seeking me out, following me all over the social media.

Confidence is magnetic. It draws people and opportunities to you like a moth to a flame. I've seen this countless times in my own journey. When I started speaking about multifamily investing with genuine confidence—not arrogance, but authentic belief in my knowledge and experience—the quality of my networking conversations transformed. People weren't just listening; they were seeking me out, following me all over the social media.

Challenge yourself: For the next week, consciously exude confidence in your interactions. Stand tall, make eye contact, speak with conviction. But here's the key—don't just focus on the external. Ground your confidence in real knowledge and preparation.

Note how people respond differently. Keep a "Confidence Impact Journal" to track the shifts you observe.

3. It Enhances Decision-Making When you trust yourself, you make decisions more quickly and decisively. In the fast-paced world of entrepreneurship, this can be a game-changer. Research shows that confident leaders make decisions 30% faster than their hesitant counterparts, and they're more likely to stick with those decisions.

Make it a habit: Next time you're faced with a decision, give yourself a time limit. Trust your gut and make the call. Remember, a good decision now is often better than a perfect decision later.

The more you practice this, the more your confidence in your decision-making abilities will grow.

4. It Boosts Resilience: Confidence gives you the strength to bounce back from setbacks. It's the voice in your head that says, "I've got this," even when things get tough. I remember when my first gas station location struggled in its early months. It wasn't my confidence in immediate success that got me through—it was my confidence in my ability to learn, adapt, and eventually succeed.

Practice this: After each setback, big or small, say to yourself, "This is temporary. I have the skills and resilience to overcome this." Make it your mantra. But don't stop there. Create what I call a "Resilience Ritual":

5. It Inspires Others: As an entrepreneur, your confidence doesn't just affect you—it influences your entire team. When you believe in yourself, others believe in you too. This creates a positive feedback loop that can transform your entire organization.

Start small: Share your vision for your business with unbridled enthusiasm. Let your confidence in your ideas shine through. Watch how it energizes those around you. But remember, true confidence isn't about pretending you have all the answers.

Remember, confidence isn't about never feeling fear—it's about feeling the fear and moving forward anyway. It's about trusting in your ability to handle whatever challenges arise. Start building your confidence today, one small action at a time. Your team, your business, and your future self will thank you.

The beauty of confidence is that it's like a muscle—the more you exercise it, the stronger it becomes. Every time you take action despite uncertainty, every time you bounce back from a setback, every time you inspire someone else to believe in themselves, you're building your confidence muscle.

So, which aspect of confidence will you focus on strengthening first? The choice is yours but remember—true confidence comes from consistent action aligned with your values and vision. Start building yours today.

Building Authentic Confidence: Where Self-Awareness Meets Self-Assurance

Now, I know what some of you are thinking. "But Kay Kay, isn't this just 'fake it till you make it'?" And here's where I'm going to challenge you - authentic confidence isn't about faking anything. It's about building real, unshakeable self-belief.

So how do you do that? Here are some strategies that have worked for me and many other successful entrepreneurs:

1. Celebrate Your Wins: No win is too small to celebrate. Each victory, no matter how tiny, is evidence of your capability.

Action Step: Start a "Win Journal". At the end of each day, write down three things you accomplished, no matter how small. Review it regularly to remind yourself of your ongoing success.

2. Embrace Your Failures: Failure isn't the opposite of confidence - it's a steppingstone to it. Each failure is an opportunity to learn and grow.

Try this: After each setback, ask yourself, "What can I learn from this? How can I use this experience to become stronger?" This shifts your mindset from defeat to growth.

3. Develop Your Skills: Confidence comes from knowing you're prepared. Continuously improving your skills gives you a solid foundation for self-belief.

Challenge yourself: Identify one skill that would significantly impact your business. Commit to spending 30 minutes each day for the next month improving that skill.

4. Practice Self-Compassion: Be kind to yourself. Treat yourself with the same compassion you'd offer a good friend who's struggling.

Make it a habit: When you catch yourself in negative self-talk, pause and ask, "Would I say this to a friend?" If not, rephrase your thoughts more compassionately.

5. Use Power Posing: Your body language affects how you feel. Research by social psychologist Amy Cuddy shows that adopting confident postures can actually make you feel more confident.

Action Step: Before your next important meeting or presentation, spend two minutes in a "power pose" - stand tall, arms raised in a V, chin up. Feel the confidence flow through you.

Vulnerability-Confidence Paradox: The Courage to Be Imperfect Unlocks True Power

Now, here's where things get really interesting. You might think that to be confident, you need to project an image of perfection and invincibility. But research by Dr. Brené Brown has shown the opposite to be true. Real, authentic confidence comes from embracing vulnerability.

Think about it. When you pretend to have it all together, people can sense the facade. But when you're honest about your struggles and imperfections, it creates a genuine connection. And here's the kicker - it actually makes you appear more confident.

I'll share a personal story with you. When I first started speaking on stage, I thought I had to project an image of flawless success. I'd talk about my wins, my strategies, my insights. But something was missing - the audience wasn't fully connecting. It wasn't until I started sharing my failures, my doubts, my moments of utter confusion, that things changed. Suddenly, the energy in the room shifted. People leaned in. They connected. And ironically, they saw me as more confident and credible.

That's the power of vulnerable confidence. It's not about pretending to be perfect - it's about being authentic and secure enough in yourself to show your imperfections.

So, how do you cultivate this kind of authentic, vulnerable confidence? Here are some strategies:

1.Share Your Journey, Not Just Your Destination: Don't just talk about your successes - share the struggles that got you there.

Try this: Next time you're talking about a business win, include the setbacks you faced along the way. Watch how it changes the way people relate to you.

2. Admit When You Don't Know: Confidence isn't about having all the answers - it's about being secure enough to admit when you don't.

Challenge yourself: Next time you're asked a question you can't answer, resist the urge to bluff. Instead, say, "That's a great question. I don't know the answer right now, but I'll find out." Watch how people respect your honesty.

3. Ask for Help: Asking for help isn't a sign of weakness - it's a sign of self-assurance and good leadership.

Make it a habit: Identify one area where you're struggling in your business. Reach out to a mentor or peer for advice. Notice how this act of vulnerability actually boosts your confidence.

4. Embrace Your Odd Habits: Your unique traits are what make you, you. Embracing them is a powerful act of self-confidence.

Action Step: List three of your odd habits or unconventional traits. Now, think about how each of these could be an asset in your business. Start intentionally leveraging these unique aspects of yourself.

5. Practice Radical Honesty: Be truthful, even when it's uncomfortable. It builds trust and, counterintuitively, makes you appear more confident.

Start small: In your next team meeting, share one thing you're currently struggling with in the business. Be honest about your concerns and uncertainties. Notice how this vulnerability actually strengthens your leadership.

Remember, building confidence is a journey, not a destination. It's about progress, not perfection. And it's absolutely crucial for your success as an entrepreneur.

So, I challenge you: For the next 30 days, commit to one confidence-building action each day. It could be as simple as striking a power pose each morning, or as challenging as sharing a vulnerable story with your team.

Will it be comfortable? Not always. Will there be moments when your confidence wavers? Absolutely. But remember why you're doing this. Remember the opportunities, the resilience, and the success that await on the other side of genuine self-belief.

You have the power to build unshakeable confidence. You have the ability to lead with both strength and vulnerability. And in doing so, you'll not only build a more successful business - but you'll also become a more authentic, impactful entrepreneur. So, are you ready to step into your confidence? Are you ready to embrace both your strengths and your vulnerabilities? The choice is yours. And I believe in you.

Let's build that confidence. Let's embrace that vulnerability. Your next level of success is waiting on the other side of your next confident action. Go take it.

Key Takeaways:

- Confidence is a skill that can be built, not an innate trait.
- Authentic confidence comes from embracing both your strengths and vulnerabilities.
- Small, daily actions can significantly boost your confidence over time.
- Confidence is crucial for risk-taking, decision-making, and inspiring others in your entrepreneurial journey.

Action Steps:

1. Start a daily "Win Journal" to celebrate your accomplishments.
2. Practice power posing before important events.
3. Share a vulnerable story about your entrepreneurial journey with your team or audience.
4. Identify and leverage one of your odd habits as a unique business asset.
5. Commit to one confidence-building action every day for the next 30 days.

Remember, as Oprah Winfrey once said, "You become what you believe." So, believe in yourself, embrace your journey, and watch as your confidence propels you to new heights of entrepreneurial success.

Chapter 11

Decision Mastery - Forging Your Entrepreneurial Destiny

> It is in your moments of decision
> that your destiny is shaped."
> - Tony Robbins

In this chapter you'll learn how decision-making becomes a critical differentiator for entrepreneurial success. It provides frameworks and techniques for making tough choices under uncertainty, while exploring how emotional intelligence and data analysis can be combined for optimal decision outcomes.

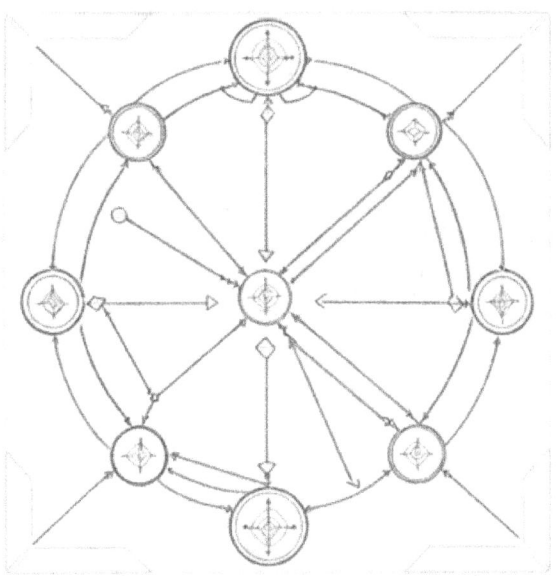

The year was 1997. Apple, once a tech darling, was on the brink of bankruptcy. The company's product line had ballooned to over 350 items, confusing customers and draining resources. Enter Steve Jobs, returning to the company he co-founded. In a bold move that would reshape Apple's future, Jobs made a decision that shocked many: he slashed the product line by 70%.

"Focusing is about saying no," Jobs declared. This decision, born from clarity and conviction, set Apple on a path to becoming the most valuable company in the world. But what separated this decision from the countless others made in boardrooms every day? What makes some choices transformative while others lead to ruin?

Let's dive into the fascinating world of decision-making and uncover how mastering this skill can be your secret weapon in entrepreneurship.

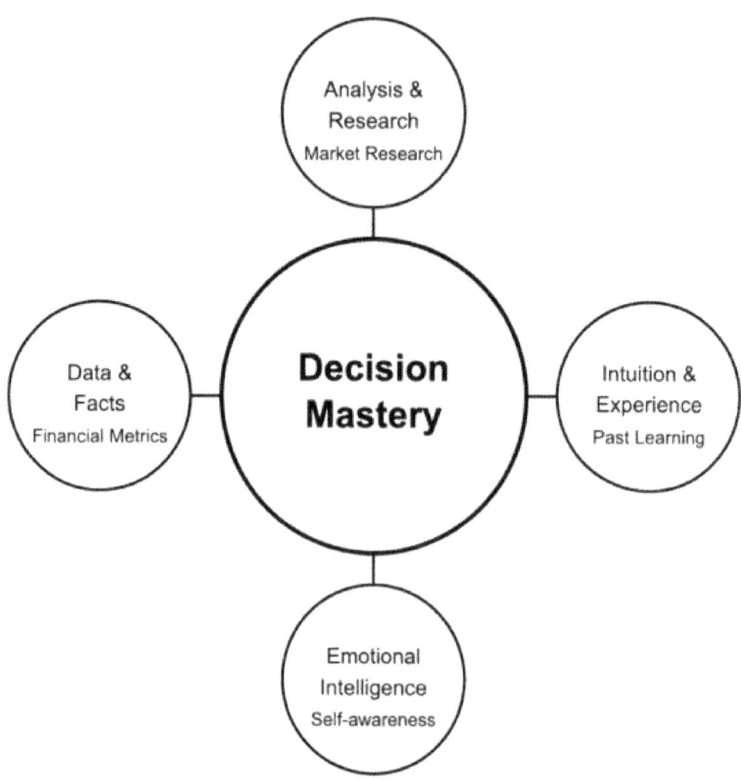

Psychology of Entrepreneurial Decisions: Decoding the Mind's Blueprint for Business Breakthroughs

Dr. Daniel Kahneman, Nobel laureate and pioneer in decision-making psychology, once said, "We're blind to our blindness. We have very little idea of how little we know. We're not designed to know how little we know."

This humbling insight is particularly relevant for entrepreneurs.

We often overestimate our ability to make good decisions, falling prey to cognitive biases that cloud our judgment. Think of these biases as invisible forces shaping your decisions—like underwater currents that can pull even the strongest swimmer off course.

Let's dive deep into these biases and learn how to navigate around them:

1. Confirmation Bias: The Echo Chamber Effect

We tend to seek out information that confirms our existing beliefs while ignoring contradictory evidence. It's like wearing rose-colored glasses that only let us see what we want to see.

2. Sunk Cost Fallacy: The Money Pit Trap

We continue investing in a failing project because we've already put so much into it. This is like continuing to pour money into a broken-down car just because you've already spent thousands on repairs.

3. Overconfidence Bias: The Superman Syndrome

We overestimate our abilities and the accuracy of our predictions. This is particularly dangerous for entrepreneurs because we need confidence to succeed, but overconfidence can lead to disaster.

4. Availability Heuristic: The "What Have You Done for Me Lately?" Effect

We give more weight to recent or easily remembered information. It's like judging a restaurant based only on your last meal there, ignoring years of previous experiences.

5. Loss Aversion: The "Bird in Hand" Paralysis

We feel the pain of losses more acutely than the pleasure of equivalent gains. This can lead to overly conservative decision-making and missed opportunities.

Remember, the goal isn't to eliminate these biases—that's impossible. The goal is to be aware of them and create systems to minimize their impact on your decision-making. Think of it like developing a GPS system for your mind—one that helps you navigate around these cognitive blind spots.

By understanding and actively working to counteract these biases, you can make clearer, more objective decisions. Remember, the most successful entrepreneurs aren't those who never face these biases—they're the ones who learn to recognize and work around them.

Your decision-making superpower isn't in avoiding biases altogether—it's in knowing they exist and having systems in place to counter them. Start building those systems today.

Understanding these biases is the first step in overcoming them. But knowledge alone isn't enough. We need frameworks and strategies to make better decisions consistently.

The 10/10/10 Framework: A Tool for Clarity

Imagine you're faced with a crucial decision: should you pivot your product strategy or stay the course? The stakes feel impossibly high. This is where the 10/10/10 framework, popularized by Suzy Welch, can be invaluable.

The 10/10/10 Decision-Making Framework

Here's how it works:

When faced with a difficult decision, ask yourself:

1. How will I feel about this decision 10 minutes from now?
2. Consider the immediate emotional impact and short-term consequences.
3. How will I feel about this decision 10 months from now?
4. Think about the medium-term effects on your business and personal life.
5. How will I feel about this decision 10 years from now?
6. Evaluate the long-term implications and alignment with your overall vision.

How to Use:

1. Write down your responses to each question.
2. Reflect on any differences between your short-term and long-term perspectives.
3. Use these insights to make a more balanced decision.
4. Remember: This framework helps you transcend immediate emotional reactions and consider the broader impact of your choices.

Action Step: Take a pending business decision and run it through the 10/10/10 framework. Write down your answers and reflect on how this changes your perspective.

The Unexpected Link: Decision-Making and Emotional Intelligence

Now, let's connect some dots that might surprise you. Now you would say "Kay Kay, what does emotional intelligence have to do with making smart business decisions? Everything, as it turns out.

Meet Sarah, a tech entrepreneur who built a promising startup from the ground up. Despite her technical brilliance, Sarah struggled with a critical weakness: she made impulsive decisions when under stress, often alienating team members and investors.

It wasn't until Sarah focused on developing her emotional intelligence that her decision-making abilities truly flourished. She learned to recognize her emotional states, manage her reactions, and empathize with others. This newfound awareness allowed her to make more balanced, thoughtful choices, even under pressure.

Research backs up Sarah's experience. A study published in the Journal of Organizational Behavior found that leaders with higher emotional intelligence made more effective decisions and achieved better business outcomes.

So, how can you harness the power of emotional intelligence in your decision-making process? Here are three strategies:

1.Practice Mindfulness: Your Mental Clarity Powerhouse

Regular meditation can help you become more aware of your thoughts and emotions, allowing you to make decisions from a place of clarity rather than reactivity. Think of mindfulness as your mental gym—just as you exercise your body for physical strength, you need to train your mind for emotional intelligence and decision-making prowess.

2.Seek Diverse Perspectives: The Power of Collective Wisdom

Actively listen to team members and stakeholders with different viewpoints. This not only improves your decisions but also builds, relationships. Think of each perspective as a unique piece of a puzzle—the more pieces you have, the clearer the full picture becomes.

3.Embrace the Pause: Your Strategic Success Buffer
When faced with a high-stakes decision, give yourself permission to pause and process. This "cooling off" period can prevent emotionally driven choices you might later regret.

Think of it as installing a circuit breaker in your decision-making process—protecting you from the power surges of emotional reactivity.

4.Power of Vulnerability in Decision-Making: Transform Doubt into Decisive Wisdom

"Vulnerability is not winning or losing; it's having the courage to show up and be seen when we have no control over the outcome." - Brené Brown

Let's talk about something that might make you squirm a little: vulnerability. In the world of entrepreneurship, vulnerability is often seen as weakness. But what if I told you that embracing vulnerability could lead to better decisions and stronger leadership?

Consider the story of Ray Dalio, founder of Bridgewater Associates, the world's largest hedge fund. Dalio attributes much of his success to a principle he calls "radical transparency." This approach involves openly sharing decision-making processes, admitting mistakes, and inviting critique from all levels of the organization.

At first glance, this level of vulnerability might seem terrifying. Won't it undermine authority? Won't competitors take advantage? But Dalio found the opposite to be true. By creating a culture where it's safe to be wrong and to learn from mistakes, Bridgewater has made better decisions and built stronger teams.

So, how can you incorporate vulnerability into your decision-making process?

1. Admit what you don't know: It's okay not to have all the answers. Acknowledging gaps in your knowledge opens the door to learning and collaboration.

2. Share your reasoning: When making a decision, explain your thought process. This invites valuable input and builds trust with your team.

3. Own your mistakes: When a decision doesn't pan out, take responsibility. Analyze what went wrong and share the lessons learned.

Remember, vulnerability in leadership isn't about being weak. It's about having the courage to be authentic, to learn publicly, and to build genuine connections with your team.

Putting It All Together: Your Decision Mastery Action Plan

You've got the knowledge. You've seen the frameworks. Now it's time to put it all into action. Here's your five-step plan to level up your decision-making skills:

1. Bias Check: Before making any significant decision, run through the list of cognitive biases we discussed. Ask yourself, "Am I falling into any of these traps?"

2. 10/10/10 Analysis: Apply the 10/10/10 framework to gain perspective on the short and long-term implications of your choice.

3. Emotional Intelligence Pause: Take a moment to check in with your emotions. Are you deciding from a place of clarity or reactivity?

4. Seek Diverse Input: Actively solicit opinions from team members with different backgrounds and viewpoints.

5. Embrace Vulnerability: Share your decision-making process openly, admit uncertainties, and be willing to course-correct if needed.

Remember, decision mastery isn't about always making the right choice. It's about developing a process that consistently leads to better outcomes over time. It's about learning from every decision, whether it leads to success or failure.

Chapter 11: Decision Mastery - Forging Your Entrepreneurial Destiny

As you implement this action plan, you'll likely face resistance - both from others and from within yourself. That's normal. Change is uncomfortable. But as Mark Manson would say, "If you're not uncomfortable, you're not growing."

So, embrace the discomfort. Lean into the challenge of improving your decision-making skills. Because here's the truth: your decisions shape your destiny as an entrepreneur. Each choice you make is a brick in the foundation of your success.

You have the power to make choices that will transform your business and your life. So, what's it going to be? Will you stick with the comfortable but limiting decisions of the past? Or will you step up, embrace these new tools, and make choices that propel you towards your dreams?

The decision, as always, is yours. Choose wisely.

Action Steps:

1. Identify the top three decisions you need to make in your business right now.
2. Apply the Decision Mastery Action Plan to each of these decisions.
3. Journal about the process and any insights you gain.
4. Share your decision-making process with a trusted advisor or mentor for feedback.
5. Commit to using this approach for all significant decisions for the next 30 days.

Key Takeaways:

- Understanding cognitive biases is crucial for making better decisions.
- The 10/10/10 framework helps balance short-term and long-term perspectives.
- Emotional intelligence plays a vital role in effective decision-making.
- Vulnerability in decision-making can lead to better outcomes and stronger teams.
- Consistent application of a decision-making process is key to long-term success.

Remember, the journey to decision mastery is ongoing. Every choice is an opportunity to learn and grow. So go forth, make bold decisions, and shape your entrepreneurial destiny.

Chapter 12

The Leadership Leap - Inspiring Others to Achieve Greatness

> "A leader is one who knows the way, goes the way, and shows the way."
> – John C. Maxwell

In this chapter you'll lean to dive into the essential elements of transformative leadership and how to inspire greatness in others. It explores the balance between strength and empathy in modern leadership, while providing practical frameworks for developing authentic leadership capabilities that motivate teams to achieve extraordinary results.

On March 15, 2019, New Zealand faced one of its darkest days. A terrorist attack on two mosques in Christchurch left 51 people dead and a nation in shock. In the midst of this crisis, a leader emerged who would redefine what it means to lead with empathy and strength.

Prime Minister Jacinda Ardern, then just 38 years old, stepped into the global spotlight. Her response? A masterclass in crisis leadership that would be studied for years to come.

Within hours of the attack, Ardern addressed the nation, her voice quivering with emotion but her message clear and resolute. "We were not chosen for this act of violence because we condone racism, because we are an enclave for extremism," she said. "We were chosen for the very fact that we are none of these things. Because we represent diversity, kindness, compassion."

In the days that followed, Ardern's leadership continued to shine. She wore a hijab when meeting with Muslim community leaders, a powerful symbol of solidarity. She refused to name the attacker, denying him the notoriety he sought. And she swiftly moved to change gun laws, showing decisive action in the face of tragedy. But it wasn't just what Ardern did that captivated the world - it was how she did it. With genuine empathy, unwavering resolve, and a touch of vulnerability that made her relatable to millions.

Ardern's leadership during this crisis exemplifies a new paradigm of leadership - one that balances strength with empathy, action with emotion, and power with vulnerability. It's a style of leadership that's becoming increasingly crucial in our complex, interconnected world. And it's a style that every entrepreneur seeking to make a lasting impact must learn to embrace.

As we dive into this chapter on leadership, keep Ardern's example in mind. Because the truth is, whether you're leading a nation through crisis or a startup through its early stages, the principles of great leadership remain the same.

The Science of Leadership: What Research Tells Us

Now, you might be thinking, "That's a great story, Kay Kay, but I'm not leading a state or a country. How does this apply to me?" Fair question. Let's look at what the science says about effective leadership in entrepreneurship.

A 2019 study published in the Journal of Business Venturing found that transformational leadership - a style characterized by inspiring and motivating followers - was positively associated with startup performance. The researchers found that leaders who could articulate a compelling vision, provide individualized support, and stimulate intellectual curiosity in their teams were more likely to lead successful ventures.

But here's where it gets interesting. The study also found that the relationship between transformational leadership and startup performance was strongest when the leader demonstrated high levels of emotional intelligence. In other words, it's not enough to be visionary and motivating - you also need to be able to understand and manage your own emotions and those of others.

This aligns perfectly with the work of Daniel Goleman, a psychologist and author who has written extensively on emotional intelligence in leadership. Goleman's research has shown that emotional intelligence accounts for 90% of what sets high performers apart from peers with similar technical skills and knowledge.

So, what does this mean for you as an entrepreneur? It means that to be an effective leader, you need to develop not just your business acumen, but also your emotional intelligence. You need to be able to inspire and motivate, yes, but also to empathize, to listen, and to connect on a human level.

The Vulnerability Factor: Brené Brown's Revolutionary Research

Now, let's talk about something that might make you uncomfortable: vulnerability. I can almost hear some of you thinking, "Vulnerability? In business? No way. I need to appear strong and confident at all times."

But what if I told you that embracing vulnerability could actually make you a more effective leader?

This is where the groundbreaking work of Brené Brown comes in. Brown, a research professor at the University of Houston, has spent two decades studying courage, vulnerability, shame, and empathy. Her findings? Vulnerability is not a weakness - it's our most accurate measure of courage.

In her book "Dare to Lead," Brown writes, "Vulnerability is the birthplace of innovation, creativity, and change." She argues that leaders who have the courage to be vulnerable - to admit when they don't have all the answers, to ask for help, to own their mistakes - are actually perceived as more authentic and trustworthy by their teams.

This isn't just feel-good rhetoric. A 2017 study published in the Journal of Applied Psychology found that when leaders were willing to be vulnerable with their teams, it led to increased psychological safety among team members. This, in turn, led to more creativity, innovation, and risk-taking - all crucial elements for entrepreneurial success.

So, how can you embrace vulnerability in your leadership? Here are a few practical steps:

1. Admit when you don't know something. Instead of pretending to have all the answers, say, "I'm not sure, but let's figure it out together."

2. Share your own struggles and challenges. This doesn't mean oversharing or being inappropriately personal but rather being honest about the difficulties you face as a leader.

3. Ask for feedback - and really listen to it. This shows that you value your team's input and are willing to grow and change.

4. Own your mistakes. When you mess up (and you will - we all do), admit it openly and focus on how to make it right.

The Power of Authentic Connections: Your Bridge to Lasting Success

Now, let's talk about something that might seem obvious, but is often overlooked in the hustle of entrepreneurship: the importance of authentic connections. In our digital age of carefully curated social media posts and polished business personas, authenticity has become not just refreshing—it's become a superpower.

In his groundbreaking book "Tribes," Seth Godin presents a fascinating perspective that's more relevant today than ever before. He argues that the internet has ended mass marketing and revived a human social unit from the distant past: tribes. Godin defines a tribe as "a group of people connected to one another, connected to a leader, and connected to an idea."

Think about that for a moment. In today's world, people aren't just buying products or services—they're joining movements, becoming part of communities, aligning themselves with values and visions that resonate with their own.

As an entrepreneur, your role is to be the leader that connects people to an idea—your vision for your company. But here's the catch, and it's a big one: people won't truly connect with you or your vision unless they perceive you as authentic. This isn't just about being "real"—it's about being consistently, unwaveringly true to your values and vision.

Let me share a personal story that drove this lesson home for me. When I first started sharing my multifamily investment journey, I thought I needed to project an image of constant success and perfect decision-making. Someone told me to fake it, until you make it approach. I would hide my struggles, downplay my challenges, and only share the wins. The result? Limited engagement and superficial connections.

But later I decided to be real and authentic. Everything changed when I started sharing the real story—the sleepless nights worrying about property acquisitions, the mistakes I made in my first multifamily deal, the lessons learned from failed negotiations. To my surprise, these vulnerable moments didn't diminish my authority—they enhanced it. People didn't just listen more; they connected more deeply.

This is where many entrepreneurs stumble. They put on a facade of infallibility, thinking it will inspire confidence. They create what I call the "Success Mask"—a perfect but artificial image of entrepreneurial achievement. But in reality, it often has the opposite effect. People can sense inauthenticity, and it erodes trust faster than any business mistake ever could.

Think about it this way: Your authenticity is like a bridge between you and your tribe. Every time you're genuine, you strengthen that bridge. Every time you're artificial, you add cracks to it.

So, how do you build authentic connections? Here are a few strategies:

1. Be transparent about your journey

Share not just your successes, but also your struggles and lessons learned. Transparency isn't just about being open—it's about creating a narrative that others can relate to and learn from. When you share your complete journey, including the stumbles and setbacks, you create a deeper connection with others. Remember, your vulnerabilities aren't weaknesses—they're bridges that connect you to others on a profound level.

2. Show genuine interest in others

Take the time to really listen to your team members, customers, and partners. This isn't just about hearing words—it's about understanding the emotions, motivations, and dreams behind them. Genuine interest means being fully present in conversations, asking thoughtful questions, and remembering what matters to others. When you demonstrate real curiosity about others' perspectives, you build relationships that go beyond surface-level interactions.

3. Be consistent in your words and actions

Nothing kills authenticity faster than saying one thing and doing another. Consistency is the backbone of trust in business relationships. It's about aligning your actions with your stated values and following through on your commitments. When your behavior consistently matches your words, you build a reputation for reliability and integrity. Remember, people are watching what you do more closely than they're listening to what you say.

4. Express gratitude

Regularly acknowledge the contributions of others to your success. Gratitude isn't just about saying "thank you"—it's about recognizing and honoring the interconnected nature of success. When you genuinely appreciate others' contributions, you create an environment of mutual support and recognition. True gratitude creates a ripple effect that strengthens relationships and builds lasting loyalty.

Chapter 12: The Leadership Leap - Inspiring Others to Achieve Greatness

Action Step: The Leadership Audit

Alright, it's time to put all this into action. I want you to conduct a personal leadership audit. Here's how:

1. Self-Assessment: Rate yourself on a scale of 1-10 on the following aspects of leadership:

   Vision and inspiration ___
   Emotional intelligence ___
   Vulnerability and authenticity ___
   Communication skills ___
   Decision-making ability ___
   Empathy and understanding ___
   Ability to develop others ___

2. Feedback: Ask at least five people who work with you (team members, partners, mentors) to rate you on the same aspects. Compare their ratings to your self-assessment.

3. Reflection: Where are the biggest gaps between your self-perception and others' perceptions? What surprises you about the feedback?

4. Development Plan: Based on your audit, identify three key areas for improvement. For each area, set a specific, measurable goal and outline the steps you'll take to achieve it.

Remember, great leadership isn't about being perfect. It's about continuous growth and a commitment to bringing out the best in yourself and others.

As you embark on this leadership journey, keep in mind the words of Simon Sinek: "Leadership is not about being in charge. Leadership is about taking care of those in your charge."

Now, go forth and lead with authenticity, vulnerability, and purpose. Your team - and your business - will thank you for it.

Key Takeaways:

1. Effective leadership balances strength with empathy, action with emotion, and power with vulnerability.
2. Emotional intelligence is crucial for leadership success in entrepreneurship.
3. Vulnerability in leadership can lead to increased trust, creativity, and innovation in your team.
4. Authentic connections are key to inspiring and motivating others.
5. Great leadership is a continuous journey of growth and self-improvement.

Remember, the greatest leaders aren't those who have all the answers. They're the ones who have the courage to ask the right questions, the humility to listen, and the resolve to take action. As you continue your entrepreneurial journey, strive to be that kind of leader. Your success - and the success of those you lead - depends on it.

Chapter 13

Focus Fundamentals - Cutting Through the Noise

> Concentrate all your thoughts upon the work at hand. The sun's rays do not burn until brought to a focus."
> - Alexander Graham Bell

In this chapter you'll learn how to develop laser-sharp focus in a world of constant distractions and competing priorities. It provides science-backed strategies for cutting through the noise and maintaining concentration on what truly matters, showing entrepreneurs how to transform their focus into a powerful competitive advantage.

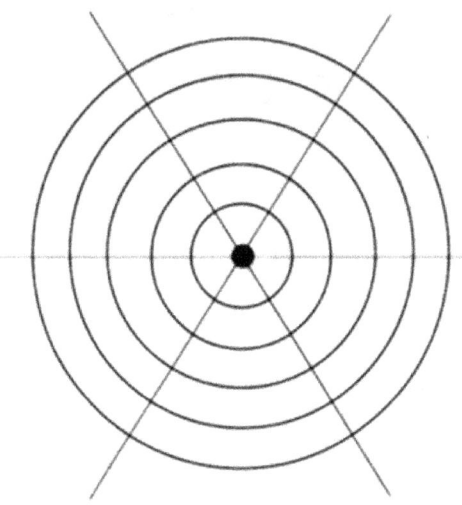

On a crisp autumn morning in 1965, a young investor named Warren Buffett sat at his desk in Omaha, Nebraska, poring over financial reports. The stock market was buzzing with activity, and countless opportunities seemed to beckon. But Buffett wasn't interested in the noise. His eyes were fixed on a single company: American Express.

The credit card giant was reeling from a scandal involving fraudulent loans, and its stock had plummeted. Most investors were fleeing, but Buffett saw something different. He recognized the enduring value of the American Express brand and its dominant position in the credit card market. While others were distracted by the chaos, Buffett maintained laser-like focus on the fundamentals.

In a bold move, he invested a staggering 40% of his partnership's assets into American Express stock. It was a bet that would pay off handsomely. Over the next few years, as the company recovered and thrived, Buffett's investment multiplied several times over, cementing his reputation as one of the most successful investors of all time.

This story illustrates a fundamental truth about entrepreneurship and success: the power of focus. In a world constantly vying for our attention, the ability to cut through the noise and concentrate on what truly matters is nothing short of a superpower.

But here's the kicker: focus isn't just about willpower or discipline. It's about understanding how your brain works and leveraging that knowledge to your advantage. Let's dive into the neuroscience of focus and discover how you can harness its power to skyrocket your productivity and decision-making.

Chapter 13: Focus Fundamentals - Cutting Through the Noise

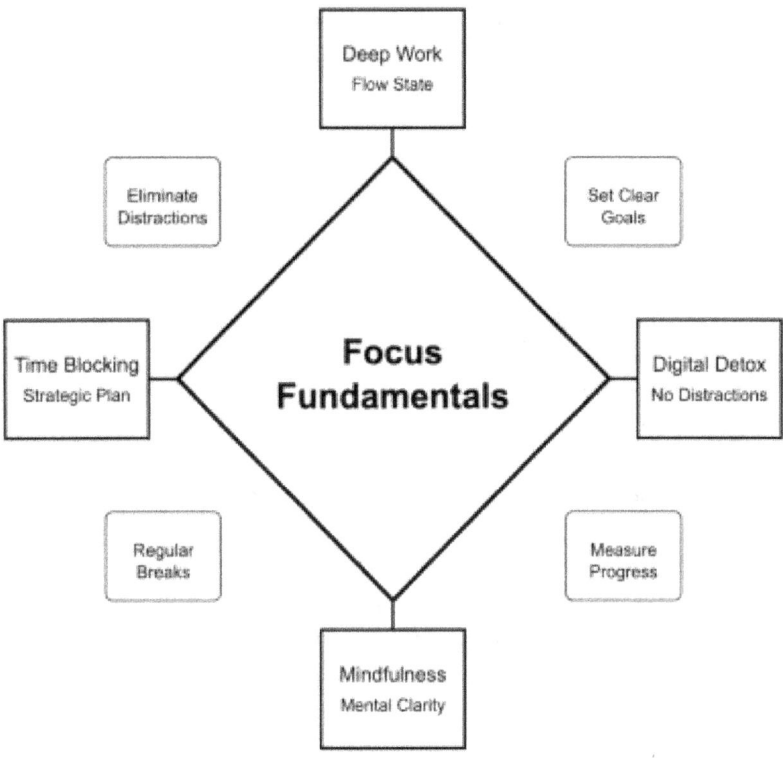

The Science of Focus

Recent studies in neuroscience have shed light on why focus is so crucial for success. A 2018 study published in the journal Nature found that when we focus intently on a task, our brains release a surge of norepinephrine, a neurotransmitter that enhances attention and information processing. This "focus boost" allows us to work more efficiently and make better decisions.

But here's the catch: our brains aren't wired for constant focus. They operate in two distinct modes: the focused mode and the diffuse mode. The focused mode is like a spotlight, illuminating a specific area with intense clarity. The diffuse mode, on the other hand, is like a floodlight, casting a wider, softer glow that allows for creative connections and problem-solving.

The key to peak performance isn't just about maximizing focus – it's about learning to toggle effectively between these two modes. This is where the magic happens.

Case Study: Elon Musk's "Time Boxing" Technique

Let's look at how another modern business titan leverages the power of focus. Elon Musk, the founder of SpaceX and Tesla, is known for his ambitious goals and relentless work ethic. But what many don't realize is that Musk's productivity secret lies in his mastery of focus.

Musk uses a technique called "time boxing," where he divides his day into five-minute blocks. Each block is assigned a specific task, and Musk focuses intensely on that task for the allotted time. This approach allows him to maintain laser-like focus while also ensuring he doesn't get bogged down in any single task.

"I think it's very important to have a feedback loop, where you're constantly thinking about what you've done and how you could be doing it better," Musk once said. This constant feedback and adjustments are a hallmark of the growth mindset, a concept pioneered by psychologist Carol Dweck.

The Growth Mindset and Focus: The Art of Turning Potential into Performance

Dweck's research has shown that individuals with a growth mindset – those who believe their abilities can be developed through dedication and hard work – are more likely to focus on learning and improvement rather than worrying about how they'll be judged. This mindset allows them to maintain focus even in the face of challenges or setbacks.

Practical Exercise: Identifying Your Mindset

Take a moment to reflect on your own mindset. Think about a recent challenge you faced in your business. How did you approach it? Did you see it as an opportunity to learn and grow, or as a threat to your abilities? Write down your thoughts and see if you can identify any fixed mindset beliefs that might be holding you back.

Now, let's talk about some practical strategies for improving your focus and avoiding the dreaded "shiny object syndrome" that plagues so many entrepreneurs.

1. The Pomodoro Technique

This time-management method involves working in focused 25-minute bursts, followed by short breaks. It's based on the idea that frequent breaks can improve mental agility.

Action Step: Try the Pomodoro Technique for one week. Use a timer to work in 25-minute focused sessions, followed by 5-minute breaks. After four "pomodoros," take a longer 15–30-minute break. Track your productivity and see how it compares to your normal work patterns.

2. Digital Detox

Our devices are constant sources of distraction. A 2018 study published in the Journal of the Association for Consumer Research found that the mere presence of a smartphone can reduce cognitive capacity, even when it's turned off. If you don't believe this, try it.

Action Step: Designate certain times of day as "phone-free" zones. Start with just 30 minutes and gradually increase. Notice how this affects your ability to focus.

3. Mindfulness Meditation

Regular mindfulness practice has been shown to increase gray matter in areas of the brain associated with focus and attention. A

2011 study published in the Proceedings of the National Academy of Sciences found that just 11 hours of meditation training can lead to structural changes in the brain that improve focus.

Action Step: Start with just 5 minutes of mindfulness meditation each day. Focus on your breath, and when your mind wanders (which it will), gently bring your attention back. Gradually increase the duration as you get more comfortable.

The Focus-Creativity Paradox: When Boundaries Become Gateways to Innovation

Now, here's where things get interesting. You might think that intense focus and creativity are at odds with each other. After all, doesn't creativity require a certain amount of mental wandering? But research suggests that the relationship between focus and creativity is more nuanced than we might expect.

A 2019 study published in the journal Neuropsychologia found that individuals who were able to focus intensely also showed higher levels of creative thinking. The researchers theorized that the ability to focus allows for deeper exploration of ideas, leading to more innovative solutions.

This aligns with the experiences of many successful entrepreneurs. Take Sara Blakely, the founder of Spanx. Blakely credits much of her success to her ability to focus intensely on solving problems. "I think one of my strengths is that I don't have a lot of preconceived notions," she once said. "I'm not afraid to fail. I will not hesitate to go down a path and do something if I believe in it."

But here's the catch: creativity also requires periods of unfocused thought. This is where the diffuse mode of thinking comes into play. By alternating between periods of intense focus and relaxed, open-ended thinking, you can maximize both your productivity and your creativity.

Practical Exercise: The Focus-Diffuse Toggle

Try this exercise to harness the power of both focused and diffuse thinking:

1. Choose a problem or challenge you're currently facing in your business.
2. Set a timer for 25 minutes and focus intensely on the problem, brainstorming potential solutions.
3. When the timer goes off, step away from your work. Go for a walk, take a shower, or engage in some other relaxing activity.
4. Notice any new ideas or insights that come to you during this "diffuse" period.
5. Return to your work and spend another focused session developing these new ideas.

The Vulnerability of Focus: The Courage to Stay Present in a World of Noise

Now, let's talk about something that often gets overlooked when discussing focus: vulnerability. As Brené Brown, renowned researcher and author, points out, allowing ourselves to be vulnerable is crucial for growth and innovation. But vulnerability can also make it harder to maintain focus, especially when we're working on something challenging or outside our comfort zone.

Personal Story: My Focus Failure

I'll share a personal story here. In 2012, I faced a defining moment in my entrepreneurial journey. With a vacant lot adjacent to my gas station and months of meticulous research indicating strong demand for a laundromat in the neighborhood, I had all the pieces in place. I'd secured the property, navigated the zoning requirements, and developed a solid business plan. Yet, as the moment of execution approached, I found myself paralyzed by an invisible force.

Instead of moving forward, I fell into a pattern of endless research—consuming laundromat podcasts, reading industry reports, and seeking more and more information. What masqueraded as "due diligence" was fear in disguise. Questions plagued my mind: Would we attract enough customers? How would I handle equipment maintenance? Each new concern became an excuse to delay action, a reason to second-guess my well-researched decision.

The breakthrough came when I recognized this pattern for what it was—fear masking itself as preparation. I realized that no amount of additional research would eliminate the inherent risks of entrepreneurship. The key wasn't to eliminate uncertainty, but to acknowledge it and move forward anyway. By refocusing on action rather than analysis, I finally broke through the paralysis and transformed my vision into reality

The lesson here? Sometimes, what looks like a focus problem is actually a vulnerability problem. By acknowledging and addressing our fears and insecurities, we can clear the mental clutter that's preventing us from focusing.

Action Step: The next time you find yourself struggling to focus, ask yourself: "What am I afraid of right now?" Write down your fears, no matter how irrational they might seem. Then, for each fear, write down a counter statement that challenges that fear. This exercise can help you move past the emotional blockages that are hindering your focus.

The Focus Myth-Buster: Where Popular Wisdom Falls, Science Prevails

Now, let's bust a common myth about focus: the idea that truly focused people work non-stop, never taking breaks or indulging in "distractions." This couldn't be further from the truth. This misconception has led countless entrepreneurs to burn themselves out, believing that any pause in their work signals weakness or lack of dedication.

In fact, research shows that taking regular breaks is crucial for maintaining focus over the long term. A 2011 study published in Cognition found that brief diversions from a task can dramatically improve one's ability to focus on that task for prolonged periods. This isn't just academic theory—it's how our brains are wired to function. The research reveals that our minds naturally oscillate between periods of intense focus and necessary recovery, much like the rhythm of our heartbeat or the pattern of our breathing.

Think of your focus like a muscle. Just as you wouldn't expect to lift weights for hours on end without rest, you can't maintain intense focus indefinitely without breaks. Trying to push through without rest doesn't make you more productive—it makes you less effective and more prone to errors. Your brain, like any high-performance tool, requires periods of rest to maintain its edge. The key is to make these breaks intentional and rejuvenating, rather than falling into the trap of mindless scrolling or busy-work.

The most successful entrepreneurs aren't those who work the longest hours without breaks—they're the ones who understand how to harness their focus in strategic bursts, followed by purposeful recovery periods. This rhythm of work and rest isn't a sign of weakness; it's a mark of wisdom. It's about working smarter, not just harder, and understanding that sustainable success requires sustainable practices.

Remember, the goal isn't to focus for as long as possible—it's to maintain high-quality focus when it matters most. Quality of attention always trumps quantity of time spent. By embracing strategic breaks, you're not reducing your productivity; you're optimizing it for the long run.

So let go of the guilt associated with taking breaks. Instead, see them as what they truly are: essential components of peak performance and sustainable success. Your ability to focus isn't measured by how long you can work without a break, but by how effectively you can direct your attention when it matters most.

Action Step: The Next-Action Break

Instead of checking your phone or email during breaks, try this: Before you step away from your work, write down the next action you'll take when you return. This keeps your subconscious mind working on the task while you rest, making it easier to refocus when you come back.

Wrapping Up: The Focus Formula

As we conclude this chapter, let's recap the key elements of the focus formula:

1. Understand the neuroscience: Your brain has focused and diffuse modes. Learn to leverage both.
2. Cultivate a growth mindset: See challenges as opportunities to learn and grow.
3. Use practical techniques: Tools like the Pomodoro Technique can enhance your focus.
4. Embrace vulnerability: Acknowledge and address the fears that may be hindering your focus.
5. Take strategic breaks: Rest is crucial for sustained focus.

Remember, developing razor-sharp focus is not about becoming a productivity robot. It's about aligning your attention with your values and goals, cutting through the noise to focus on what truly matters.

In the words of Bruce Lee, "The successful warrior is the average man, with laser-like focus." You have the power to develop this focus. It's not about who you are, but who you choose to become.

Key Takeaways

- Focus isn't about doing more things - it's about doing the right things longer.

Chapter 13: Focus Fundamentals - Cutting Through the Noise

- Your brain works best when alternating between focused and diffuse modes of thinking.
- Digital distractions don't just waste time - they fundamentally impair your cognitive capacity.
- Setting boundaries and constraints can actually enhance focus rather than limit it.
- The quality of your attention matters more than the quantity of time spent.

So, what will you focus on today? The choice is yours. Now go forth and conquer, one focused moment at a time.

Chapter 14

The Balance Beam - Thriving in Work and Life

> Happiness is not a matter of
> intensity but of balance, order,
> rhythm and harmony."
> - Thomas Merton

Having built multiple successful businesses while maintaining strong family bonds, I'll show you why the "hustle 24/7" mentality is a dangerous myth. Drawing from my own hard-learned lessons and extensive research, this chapter reveals practical strategies for achieving sustainable success without burning out or sacrificing what matters most in life.

Arianna Huffington was at the pinnacle of her career. As the co-founder and editor-in-chief of The Huffington Post, she was a media mogul, a recognized influencer, and by all conventional measures, wildly successful. But on April 6, 2007, success came at a price she wasn't prepared to pay.

Exhausted from working 18-hour days, seven days a week, Huffington collapsed in her office, hitting her head on her desk and breaking her cheekbone. As she came to in a pool of her own blood, Huffington had an epiphany: this was not what success should look like.

"By any sane definition of success, if you are lying in a pool of blood on your office floor, you are not successful," Huffington later wrote. This moment became her wake-up call, leading her to reevaluate her priorities and ultimately sparking a global conversation about work-life balance and well-being.

Huffington's story isn't unique in the entrepreneurial world. Many of us have bought into the myth that success requires sacrifice - of our time, our health, our relationships. We wear our 80-hour workweeks like badges of honor, mistaking exhaustion for dedication.

But here's the truth bomb I'm about to drop on you: that "hustle 24/7" mentality? It's not good. And it's not just bad for you - it's bad for your business too.

Let's break this down with some cold, hard facts. A 2018 study published in the Harvard Business Review found that entrepreneurs who maintained a healthy work-life balance were 10% more likely to succeed in their ventures than those who didn't. Another study from the Journal of Business Venturing showed that entrepreneurs who prioritized their well-being reported 22% higher life satisfaction and 17% lower stress levels, which directly correlated with better business performance. In other words, balance isn't just some feel-good concept - it's a crucial factor in your success as an entrepreneur.

Chapter 14: The Balance Beam - Thriving in Work and Life

Now, I can hear some of you thinking, "But Kay Kay, I've got a million things to do. I can't afford to take time off!" And trust me, I get it. I've been there. But here's the thing: working longer hours doesn't always mean better results. In fact, it often leads to low quality work and diminishing returns.

A Stanford study found that productivity per hour declines sharply when a person works more than 50 hours a week. After 55 hours, productivity drops so much that putting in any more hours would be pointless. Let that sink in for a moment. Those extra hours you're putting in. They might be doing more harm than good.

So how do we strike this elusive balance? How do we build thriving businesses without sacrificing our well-being and lifetime? Let's dive in.

1. Redefine Success: First things first, we need to change how we think about success. Success isn't just about the bottom line - it's about creating a life that's fulfilling both in and out of work.

Exercise: Take a moment to write down your definition of success. Now, ask yourself: Does this definition include your health? Your relationships? Your personal growth? If not, it's time for a rewrite.

2. Set Boundaries: Boundaries aren't just good for you - they're good for business. They help you manage your energy, increase your productivity, and avoid burnout.

Action Step: Establish clear work hours and stick to them. When you're off, be fully off. When you're on, be fully on. Communicate these boundaries to your team and clients.

3. Prioritize Self-Care: Self-care isn't selfish - it's essential. It's about maintaining your most valuable business asset: you.

Challenge: For the next 30 days, commit to one self-care activity each day. It could be gratitude, meditation, exercise, reading for pleasure - anything that recharges you. Track how it affects your energy and productivity.

4. Practice Mindfulness: Mindfulness isn't just for yogis. It's a powerful tool for entrepreneurs too, helping you stay focused, manage stress, and make better decisions.

Try This: Download a mindfulness app like Headspace or Calm. Start with just 5 minutes of mindfulness practice each day and gradually increase.

5. Learn to Delegate: You can't do it all, and you shouldn't try. Effective delegation isn't just about freeing up your time - it's about empowering your team and focusing on what you do best.

Exercise: List all your tasks for the week. Now, circle the ones that only you can do. Everything else is a candidate for delegation to your team or even virtual assistants.

6. Use Technology Wisely: Technology can be a double-edged sword. Use it to increase efficiency, not to tether yourself to work 24/7.

Action Step: Do a tech audit. Are your apps and tools serving you, or are they sources of stress? Delete or mute anything that's not adding value. Now you can even set screen time allowed on each app.

7. Cultivate Relationships: Strong relationships are crucial for both personal happiness and business success. Make time for the people who matter.

Challenge: Schedule one meaningful, uninterrupted conversation with a loved one or friend each week. No phones, no distractions - just genuine connection.

Now, I know what some of you might be thinking. "This all sounds great, Kay Kay, but I'm worried I'll fall behind if I take my foot off the gas." And I get it. The fear of missing out, of not doing enough, is real. But here's where we need to get real with ourselves.

Think about it this way: if you're constantly running on empty, how long can you really sustain that pace? It's like trying to drive cross-country without ever stopping for gas. You might make good time at first, but eventually, you're going to sputter to a stop in the middle of nowhere.

This isn't just theory - it's backed by science. A study published in the Academy of Management Journal found that entrepreneurs who took regular time off were more creative and innovative in their businesses. They came back to work with charged with fresh perspectives and new ideas.

But don't just take my word for it. Let's look at another entrepreneur who learned this lesson the hard way.

Elon Musk, the poster child for the "work yourself to the bone" mentality, famously claimed to work 120 hours a week during Tesla's Model 3 ramp-up even sleeping in a tent at the plant. The result? In his own words, "It was excruciating... It hurts my brain and heart." He admitted that this unsustainable pace affected his health and happiness, and potentially hurt Tesla.

Contrast this with Jeff Bezos, who, despite running one of the world's largest companies, prioritizes sleep and family time. Bezos is known for getting 8 hours of sleep each night and blocking out time for breakfast with his family. He credits this balance with helping him make better decisions and stay energized.

The lesson? Balance isn't a luxury - it's a necessity for long-term success.

So, how do we put all this into practice? Here's your action plan:

1. Conduct a Life Audit: Take stock of all areas of your life - work, health, relationships, personal growth. Rate your satisfaction in each area on a scale of 1-10.

2. Identify Imbalances: Where are the biggest gaps? Which areas are you neglecting?

3. Set Holistic Goals: Based on your audit, set goals for each area of your life. Remember, these should complement, not compete with, each other.

4. Create a Work Life Balance Scorecard: Develop a personal scorecard with key metrics for each life area. This could include things like hours of sleep, time spent with family, progress on business goals, etc.

5. Track and Adjust Your Scoreboard: Monitor your scorecard daily or weekly. Use this data to adjust as needed.

Remember, balance isn't about perfect equilibrium all the time. It's about being intentional with your time and energy and making sure you're nurturing all aspects of your life.

Here's a hard truth: Your business can only be as healthy as you are. This isn't just motivational speak—it's a fundamental principle of sustainable entrepreneurship. Your business is a direct reflection of your energy, clarity, and vitality. By prioritizing balance, you're not just improving your personal life - you're setting your business up for long-term, sustainable success. Think of it as investing in your business's most valuable asset: you.

So, I challenge you: For the next 30 days, commit to prioritizing balance. This isn't about dramatic lifestyle changes or abandoning your ambitions. It's about making conscious choices that honor both your business goals and your personal wellbeing. Set clear boundaries that protect your energy. Schedule time for self-care and relationships with the same commitment you give to business meetings. Pay attention to how these changes affect both your personal life and your business. Watch how your decision-making improves, how your creativity flourishes, and how your leadership strengthens when you're operating from a place of balance.

Will it be easy? Not always. The demands of entrepreneurship will continue to pull at you. Will there be times when you're tempted to fall back into old habits? Absolutely. The siren song of "just one more hour" or "just this one time" will call to you. But remember why you're doing this. Remember that sustainable success isn't about short-term sprints—it's about maintaining a steady, powerful pace for the long run. Remember the energy, the creativity, and the overall quality of life that await on the other side of true balance. This isn't just about survival; it's about thrival.

You have the power to create a thriving business without sacrificing your well-being. This isn't a pipe dream, or a luxury reserved for others—it's your birthright as an entrepreneur. You have the ability to be a successful entrepreneur and a happy, well-rounded human being. These aren't mutually exclusive goals—they're mutually reinforcing ones. And in doing so, you'll not only build a more sustainable business - but you'll also create a life you truly love living. A life that energizes rather than depletes you, that expands rather than constrains you.

So, are you ready to step on to the balance beam? Are you ready to say goodbye to burnout and hello to sustainable success? The choice, as always, is yours. And I believe in you. I believe in your capacity to build something extraordinary without sacrificing what matters most. I believe in your ability to redefine success on your own terms.

Let's create that balance. Let's build success that doesn't come at the cost of our health or relationships. This isn't about choosing between business success and personal fulfillment—it's about creating a life where both can flourish together. Your best life and your best business are waiting on the other side of balance. They're not separate destinations—they're part of the same journey.

Go create them. Not tomorrow, not when things slow down, not when you've reached your next business milestone—but today. Right now. Because the life you dream of, the success you envision, they begin with the choices you make in this moment.

Your journey to balanced success starts now. Take that first step. Make that first choice. Your future self will thank you.

I'll share a personal pivotal moment from my entrepreneurial journey that fundamentally changed my perspective on work-life balance. In 2022, I faced a classic entrepreneur's dilemma that taught me a powerful lesson about work-life balance. After acquiring three laundromats and a dry-cleaning plant that hadn't been renovated since 1986, I made the ambitious decision to modernize everything at once. While most laundromat owners prefer minimal reinvestment to maintain cash flow, I chose to completely overhaul the operations - replacing all coin-operated machines with modern card-operated equipment.

The six-month renovation consumed me entirely. I was on-site from dawn until late at night, seven days a week. My gym routine disappeared, family time became non-existent, and evenings consisted of collapsing on the couch before dinner and bed. The physical and mental exhaustion was unlike anything I'd experienced in my decades of entrepreneurship.

The wake-up call came when I finally completed the renovations. Looking in the mirror, I barely recognized the person I'd become. It was not just a physical impact but also a mental impact. Right then, I made a decision that would reshape my approach to business and life: I handed the keys to my son and took a week-long vacation - my first real break in about a year. This forced disconnect became my turning point. Upon returning, I deliberately reset to my pre-renovation routine, prioritizing family time, self-care, and delegation.

Chapter 14: The Balance Beam - Thriving in Work and Life

Action Step

Create your personal Balance Scorecard and track it for the next 30 days. Include metrics for work productivity, personal relationships, health, and personal growth. Review weekly and adjust as needed.

Key Takeaways:

- Work-life balance is crucial for long-term entrepreneurial success.
- Overworking leads to diminishing returns and can harm both you and your business.
- Balance isn't about perfect equilibrium, but about intentional time and energy management.
- Self-care and boundary-setting are essential business strategies, not luxuries.
- Regular self-assessment and adjustment are key to maintaining balance.

Remember, the goal isn't perfection - it's progress. Every step you take towards balance is a step towards sustainable success. You've got this. Now go show the world what a balanced, thriving entrepreneur can achieve.

Chapter 15

Adaptability - Your Competitive Edge in a Changing World

> It is not the strongest of the species that survive, nor the most intelligent, but the one most responsive to change."
> - Charles Darwin

In this essential chapter, I share how adaptability became my secret weapon in building successful businesses across multiple industries. Through real-world examples and proven strategies, I demonstrate why the ability to pivot and evolve isn't just about survival—it's about seizing hidden opportunities that others miss when markets and technologies shift.

Picture this: It's 1997, and you're walking into your local Blockbuster video store on a Friday night. The smell of popcorn fills the air, and you're surrounded by rows upon rows of VHS tapes and DVDs. You grab the latest release, pay your rental fee, and head home for movie night. Life is good.

Now, fast forward to 2007. A small company called Netflix is quietly revolutionizing the way we consume entertainment. They've just launched their streaming service, allowing subscribers to watch movies and TV shows instantly on their computers. Meanwhile, Blockbuster is still banking on their brick-and-mortar stores, seemingly oblivious to the shift happening in their industry.

We all know how this story ends. By 2010, Blockbuster filed a bankruptcy, while Netflix soared to become a global entertainment powerhouse. The difference? Adaptability.

Netflix's journey from DVD-by-mail service to streaming giant is a masterclass in adaptability. They didn't just react to change; they anticipated it, embraced it, and used it to redefine an entire industry. This, my fellow entrepreneurs, is the power of adaptability - and it's a superpower you need to cultivate if you want to thrive in today's fast-paced business world.

Now, I know what some of you might be thinking. "Kay Kay, I've got my business model figured out. Why fix what isn't broken?" But here's the truth bomb I'm about to drop on you: in business, what isn't broken today might be obsolete tomorrow. The ability to adapt isn't just nice to have - it's essential for survival and success.

Let's dive into the science behind adaptability. A 2021 study published in the Journal of Business Venturing found that entrepreneurs with high adaptability were 32% more likely to succeed in volatile markets compared to their less adaptable peers. The researchers attributed this to what they called "adaptive cognition" - the ability to quickly process new information, challenge existing assumptions, and adjust strategies accordingly.

Chapter 15: Adaptability - Your Competitive Edge in a Changing World

But here's where it gets really interesting. The study also found that adaptability isn't just about reacting to change - it's about proactively seeking it out. The most successful entrepreneurs in the study were those who actively looked for ways to innovate and evolve, even when things were going well.

This brings us to an unexpected connection: adaptability and innovation are two sides of the same coin. Think about it. To innovate, you need to be open to new ideas and willing to challenge the status quo. That's essentially what adaptability is all about.

Take Elon Musk, for example. When he co-founded PayPal, he didn't stop and say, "Great, I've revolutionized online payments. My work here is done." Instead, he looked at other industries ripe for disruption. He adapted his innovative mindset to tackle electric cars with Tesla, space exploration with SpaceX, and sustainable energy with SolarCity. That's adaptability and innovation working hand in hand.

Now, I can hear some of you saying, "But Kay Kay, I'm not Elon Musk. I don't have his resources or his genius-level IQ." And you're right, you're not Elon Musk. You're you. And that's your superpower.

Here's the thing: adaptability isn't about being a genius or having unlimited resources. It's about mindset. And the good news? Mindset can be developed.

Dr. Carol Dweck, renowned psychologist and author of "Mindset: The New Psychology of Success," has shown through decades of research that our beliefs about our abilities have a profound impact on our success. She distinguishes between a fixed mindset (believing our abilities are static) and a growth mindset (believing our abilities can be developed).

Entrepreneurs with a growth mindset see challenges as opportunities to learn and grow. They're more likely to persist in the face of setbacks, seek out feedback, and embrace change. In other words, they're more adaptable.

So, how do you cultivate this adaptable, growth-oriented mindset? Here are some strategies backed by research and real-world success stories:

1. Embrace Continuous Learning: Jeff Bezos, founder of Amazon, is famous for his "Day 1" philosophy. He operates as if every day is Day 1 of a startup, maintaining a beginner's mindset and a hunger for learning. This approach has allowed Amazon to adapt from an online bookstore to an e-commerce giant, cloud computing leader, and beyond.

Action Step: Commit to learning something new about your industry every day. Set up Google Alerts for key trends, subscribe to industry newsletters, or dedicate 30 minutes daily to reading relevant books or articles.

2. Challenge Your Assumptions: Reed Hastings, co-founder of Netflix, regularly challenges his own assumptions about the business. This led to Netflix's pivotal shift from DVD rentals to streaming, and later to producing original content.

Exercise: List your top three assumptions about your business or industry. Now, for each one, ask yourself: "What if the opposite were true?" This mental exercise can help you spot potential disruptions before they happen.

3. Seek Diverse Perspectives: Studies have shown that diverse teams are more innovative and adaptable. They bring different viewpoints and experiences, leading to more creative problem-solving. This isn't just feel-good corporate speak—it's a powerful business truth backed by extensive research. When you bring together people with different perspectives, experiences, and backgrounds, you create a dynamic environment where innovation naturally flourishes. Think of it like a rich ecosystem where various elements interact to create something greater than the sum of its parts. In today's rapidly evolving business landscape, this diversity of thought and experience isn't just a nice-to-have—it's a crucial competitive advantage that can set your business apart and drive sustainable success.

Action Step: Next time you're facing a business challenge, gather insights from people outside your immediate circle. This could be employees from different departments, mentors from other industries, or even customers.

4. Practice Scenario Planning: Scenario planning involves imagining different possible futures for your business and industry. It helps you anticipate changes and develop contingency plans. This isn't about predicting the future with perfect accuracy—it's about preparing your mind and your business for various possibilities. Think of it as creating a strategic GPS that can help you navigate no matter which road the future takes. By regularly engaging in scenario planning, you develop a more flexible and resilient mindset, one that's ready to adapt and thrive in any business climate. Instead of being caught off guard by change, you're mentally prepared with well-thought-out responses to different situations. This practice transforms you from a reactive business owner into a proactive strategist, ready to seize opportunities and mitigate risks before they fully materialize.

Exercise: Imagine three possible scenarios for your industry five years from now - one optimistic, one pessimistic, and one wildcard. How would your business need to adapt in each scenario?

5. Cultivate Emotional Intelligence: Adaptability isn't just about strategy - it's also about managing your own emotions and those of your team during times of change. This is where emotional intelligence comes in. Think of it as your internal navigation system for steering through the turbulent waters of business transformation. While strategic thinking helps you plot the course, emotional intelligence ensures you can actually navigate the journey, keeping both yourself and your team steady through the waves of change.

A study published in the Journal of Small Business Management found that entrepreneurs with high emotional intelligence were better able to adapt to market changes and lead their teams through uncertainty. This isn't surprising when you think about it—change creates emotional ripples throughout an organization, and your ability to read and respond to these emotions can make the difference between successful adaptation and failed transformation. It's not just about having a good plan; it's about having the emotional awareness and skill to execute that plan while bringing your team along with you.

Action Step: Next time you face a setback, practice the "Name it to Tame it" technique. Simply naming your emotions (e.g., "I'm feeling frustrated and scared") can help you manage them more effectively.

Now, let's talk about vulnerability. I know, I know. Vulnerability doesn't sound like something you want to cultivate as an entrepreneur. But hear me out.

Brené Brown, researcher and author of "Daring Greatly," defines vulnerability as "uncertainty, risk, and emotional exposure." Sound familiar? That's pretty much the job description of an entrepreneur.

Brown's research has shown that vulnerability is not a weakness - it's a strength. It's the birthplace of innovation, and change. All things that are crucial for adaptability.

I'll share a personal story. A few years ago, I was faced with a major decision in my business. A new competitor had entered the Laundromat market with a radically different approach and doing crazy promotion and started a price war which effected our business. My team was split on how to respond. Some wanted to stick to our guns, while others pushed for a complete overhaul of our marketing and promotion strategy.

I felt torn. On one hand, I was confident in our existing approach. On the other, I could see the potential in this new direction. I was afraid of making the wrong choice and letting my team down.

Instead of pretending I had all the answers, I decided to be vulnerable. I called a team meeting and openly shared my doubts and fears. I asked for everyone's input, admitting that I didn't have a clear solution.

Chapter 15: Adaptability - Your Competitive Edge in a Changing World

You know what happened? That vulnerability opened a flood of creativity. Team members who had been quiet before started sharing ideas. We had honest discussions about our strengths and weaknesses of programs and our strategies. And together, we came up with a hybrid approach that ended up being more successful than our original strategy or our competitor's.

That experience taught me a valuable lesson: vulnerability and adaptability go hand in hand. When you're willing to admit you don't have all the answers, you open yourself up to new possibilities.

So, here's my challenge to you: In the next week, find one opportunity to be vulnerable with your team. Share a doubt you're having, ask for help with a problem you're struggling with, or admit a mistake you've made. Watch how this openness can foster trust, creativity, and adaptability in your team.

Now, let's get real for a moment. All this talk about adaptability, growth mindsets, and vulnerability might sound great in theory. But in the trenches of entrepreneurship, it's not always easy to maintain this mindset. There will be days when you feel stuck, scared, or just plain exhausted.

On those days, remember this: adaptability is not about being perfect. It's not about always making the right choice or never feeling fear. It's about being willing to take that step forward, even when you're not sure where it will lead.

In the words of Mark Manson, author of "The Subtle Art of Not Giving a F*ck": "If you're stuck on a problem, don't sit there and think about it; just start working on it. Even if you don't know what you're doing, the simple act of working on it will eventually cause the right ideas to show up in your head."

This no-nonsense approach to adaptability is crucial. Because here's the hard truth: the market doesn't care about your feelings. It doesn't care if you're tired or scared or unsure or exhausted. It will keep changing, with or without you.

Your job as an entrepreneur is not to predict the future or to always be right. Your job is to stay in the game. To keep learning, keep growing, keep adapting.

Chapter 15: Adaptability - Your Competitive Edge in a Changing World

So, let's wrap this up with some concrete action steps:

1. Adaptability Audit: Rate yourself on a scale of 1-10 on the following aspects of adaptability:

   - Openness to new ideas ___
   - Willingness to challenge assumptions ___
   - Ability to pivot quickly ___
   - Comfort with uncertainty ___
   - Resilience in the face of setbacks ___

2. Identify Your Adaptation Anchors: What are three core values or principles that will remain constant for you, no matter how much your business changes? These will be your anchors in times of change.

3. Create an Adaptation Playbook: Based on what you've learned in this chapter, create a step-by-step plan for how you'll respond the next time you face a major change in your industry.

4. Schedule Regular Adaptation Check-ins: Set a recurring calendar reminder to assess your business's adaptability. This could be monthly, quarterly, or whatever timeline makes sense for your industry.

5. Practice Micro-Adaptations: Challenge yourself to make one small change in your routine or business practices each week. This will help build your adaptability muscle.

6. Keep yourself updated on Adaptation: Always keep updating yourself about the changes in your industry by subscribing to newsletters or magazines, attending seminars and reading about the latest changes in your industry.

Remember, adaptability is not a destination - it's a journey. It's about cultivating a mindset that embraces change, seeks out new possibilities, and isn't afraid to take calculated risks.

As you move forward in your entrepreneurial journey, keep this quote from Charles Darwin in mind: "It is not the strongest of the species that survive, nor the most intelligent, but the one most responsive to change."

Your ability to adapt could be the difference between thriving and merely surviving in the ever-changing world of business. So, embrace change, stay curious, and keep pushing forward. Your next big breakthrough might be just around the corner.

Now go forth and adapt, my fellow entrepreneurs. The future is waiting for you to shape it.

Key Takeaways:

- Adaptability is crucial for entrepreneurial success in today's fast-changing business landscape.
- A growth mindset is the foundation of adaptability.
- Vulnerability and adaptability are interconnected - being open about uncertainties can lead to innovative solutions.
- Adaptability and innovation go hand in hand - both require openness to new ideas and a willingness to challenge the status quo.
- Practicing adaptability is an ongoing process that involves continuous learning, challenging assumptions, and embracing change.

Remember, the most successful entrepreneurs aren't necessarily the smartest or the most experienced - they're the ones who can adapt most effectively to change. So, keep learning, stay flexible, and never stop evolving. Your adaptability is your competitive edge. Use it wisely.

Chapter 16

The Delegation Revelation - Unleashing Your Team's Potential

> The best executive is the one who has sense enough to pick good men to do what he wants done, and self-restraint to keep from meddling with them while they do it."
> - Theodore Roosevelt

After decades of hands-on business ownership, I've learned that effective delegation is the key that unlocks true entrepreneurial freedom. In this transformative chapter, I share my journey from micromanager to empowering leader, revealing proven strategies for building a self-running business that thrives even when you're not there.

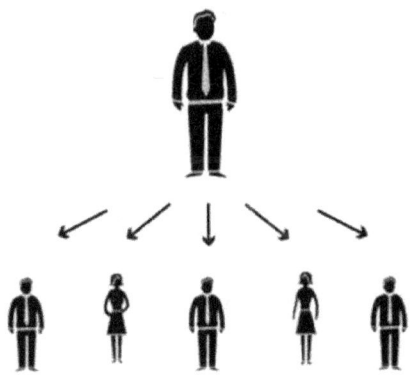

As the sun rose over a small restaurant in San Bernardino, California, in 1954, a 52-year-old milkshake machine salesman named Ray Kroc stood in awe. He watched as the McDonald brothers' revolutionary assembly-line food preparation system churned out order after order with breathtaking efficiency. Little did Kroc know that this moment would not only change his life but also revolutionize the fast-food industry worldwide.

Kroc's journey from that pivotal moment to building a global empire hinged on one crucial skill: delegation. As we delve into this chapter, we'll explore how Kroc's ability to entrust others with key responsibilities transformed a single restaurant into a worldwide phenomenon, and how you can apply these same principles to skyrocket your own entrepreneurial success.

The Psychology of Letting Go: Transform Control into Collective Excellence

Dr. Carol Dweck, renowned psychologist and author of "Mindset: The New Psychology of Success," has extensively studied the impact of mindset on achievement. Her research reveals a striking parallel between those with a growth mindset and successful delegators. Both share a fundamental belief: that abilities can be developed through dedication and hard work. This isn't just academic theory—it's a powerful framework for understanding why some entrepreneurs thrive through delegation while others remain trapped in the cycle of micromanagement.

For many entrepreneurs, delegation feels like relinquishing control. It triggers our deepest insecurities, touching the raw nerves of our entrepreneurial identity. What if they don't do it as well as I would? What if they make mistakes? What if I become redundant? These questions aren't just about tasks and efficiency—they're about our sense of self-worth and purpose. Every time we consider delegating, we're not just making a business decision; we're confronting our own relationship with control, perfection, and identity.

These fears stem from what Dweck calls a "fixed mindset" – the belief that our qualities are carved in stone. But here's the kicker: holding onto this mindset is like trying to build a skyscraper with your bare hands. It's not just inefficient; it's impossible. You might be able to lay a few bricks, but you'll never reach the heights your business can achieve. True growth, true scale, true success—they all require the ability to let go and trust others to carry part of your vision forward. This isn't about diminishing your role; it's about expanding your impact through the multiplying power of delegation. As an entrepreneur you should be working on the business not in the business.

Action Step: Identify Your Delegation Mindset

Take a moment to reflect on your current attitude towards delegation. On a scale of 1-10, how comfortable are you with handing over tasks to others? What beliefs or fears might be holding you back?

The Unexpected Connection: Delegation and Personal Growth

Now, let's take an unexpected detour into the world of ecology. In 1969, ecologist Garrett Hardin introduced the concept of "The Tragedy of the Commons." It describes a situation where individuals, acting independently and rationally according to their own self-interest, ultimately deplete a shared resource, even when it's clear that it's not in anyone's long-term interest for this to happen.

Surprisingly, this concept has a powerful parallel in the world of entrepreneurship. When we refuse to delegate, we're depleting our most precious resource: ourselves. We become the overgrazing cattle, trampling our own potential for growth and innovation. Brad Sugars in his book "The Real Estate Coach" expands on his definition of a true business as "a commercial, profitable enterprise that works without you." He emphasizes that a true business should be able to operate independently of its owner.

But here's where it gets really interesting. When we delegate effectively, we're not just freeing up our time. We're creating a thriving ecosystem of skills, ideas, and leadership within our organization. We're transforming the tragedy of the commons into a triumph of collaboration.

Ray Kroc understood this intuitively. He didn't try to run every McDonald's himself. Instead, he created a system where franchisees could operate their own restaurants while adhering to strict quality standards. This approach allowed for rapid expansion while maintaining consistency – a key factor in McDonald's global success.

The Vulnerability Factor: Embracing Imperfection

Let's get real for a moment. Delegation isn't just about efficiency; it's about vulnerability. It's about admitting that we can't do it all, and that's okay. In fact, it's more than okay – it's essential for growth.

Brené Brown, renowned researcher and author, argues that vulnerability is the birthplace of innovation, creativity, and change. When we delegate, we're showing vulnerability. We're saying, "I trust you with this important task." And in doing so, we create space for others to rise to the challenge, to innovate, to surprise us with their capabilities.

Let me share a personal pivotal moment in my entrepreneurial journey. I recall the nerve-wracking decision to hand over the daily operations of my multi-business portfolio—gas stations, convenience stores, and laundromats—to my 24-year-old son. After decades of personally overseeing every detail, this transition felt like letting go of my life's work. I had built these businesses from the ground up as an immigrant entrepreneur, and my hands-on management style was deeply ingrained in their success. The questions kept me awake at night: Would he maintain the high standards I'd established? Could he handle the complex dynamics of multiple businesses?

The result? He wasn't perfect. There were things I would have done differently and of course better. But you know what? It was good. And more importantly, it opened a whole new world of possibilities. It allowed me to focus on high-level strategy while empowering my team to manage the operations, grow and develop new businesses. I had more time to focus on my multifamily investing business and move towards retirement.

Action Step: Embrace Imperfection

Identify one task you've been hesitant to delegate. Write down your fears about delegating this task. Then, challenge each fear with a potential positive outcome. For example:

Fear: "They won't do it exactly like I would."

Potential Positive: "They might bring a fresh perspective and improve the process."

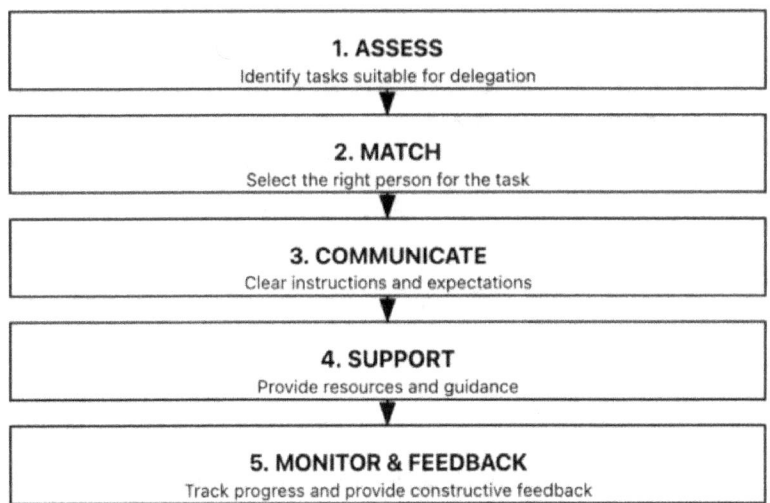

The Delegation Framework: From Theory to Practice

Now, let's get down to brass tacks. How do we actually implement effective delegation in our businesses? Here's a framework I've developed based on years of experience and research:

1. Assess: Take stock of your current workload. What tasks are eating up your time but don't require your unique skills or vision?

2. Match: Identify team members whose skills and interests align with these tasks. Remember, delegation isn't about dumping unwanted work; it's about creating opportunities for growth.

3. Communicate: Clearly articulate the task, the expected outcome, and the level of authority you're granting. Be specific about deadlines and check-in points.

4. Support: Provide the necessary resources and training. Be available for questions but resist the urge to micromanage.

5. Review: Set up regular check-ins to assess progress and provide feedback. Use these as opportunities for coaching and development.

6. Celebrate: Acknowledge successes and learn from failures. Create a culture that values initiative and learning.

Action Step: Create Your Delegation Plan

Choose three tasks to delegate this week. For each task, follow the framework above. Write out your plan for each step.

The Multiplier Effect: How Delegation Scales Your Impact

Here's a mind-bending concept: effective delegation doesn't just free up your time – it multiplies your impact exponentially.

Think about it. When you delegate, you're not just transferring tasks; you're transferring knowledge, skills, and responsibility. You're creating leaders who can, in turn, lead others.

This is the secret sauce of scaling a business. It's how Ray Kroc turned a single restaurant into a global empire. It's how Richard Branson built Virgin into a conglomerate spanning multiple industries. It's how you can take your business to the next level.

But here's the kicker: this multiplier effect doesn't just apply to your business. It applies to you as a leader. The more you delegate, the more you're forced to level up your own skills. You shift from being a doer to a strategist, from a manager to a visionary.

The Hard Truth: Delegation Isn't Optional

Now, let's cut through the hard truth. If you're serious about growing your business and avoiding burnout, delegation isn't just a nice-to-have. It's a must-have period. This isn't about preference or management style—it's about the fundamental physics of business growth. Just as there are only 24 hours in a day, there's a finite limit to what any single person can accomplish alone.

Mark Manson, author of "The Subtle Art of Not Giving a F*ck," would probably put it this way: "If you think you can do it all yourself, you're not just wrong – you're screwing yourself and your business over." A successful entrepreneur is one who doesn't work in the business but works on the business. This distinction isn't just semantic—it's the difference between being trapped in the daily grind and truly leading your organization to new heights.

Every task you insist on doing yourself is a task that's holding you back from bigger, more important work. It's like insisting on mowing your own lawn when you could be designing the next skyscraper. This isn't about capability—you might be the best lawnmower in the world—it's about opportunity cost. Every minute you spend on tasks that could be delegated is a minute you're not spending on strategic thinking, relationship building, or business development. In the unforgiving mathematics of business growth, this isn't just inefficient—it's unsustainable.

Remember: The size of your business will always be limited by your unwillingness to delegate. You can either be the bottleneck that constrains your company's growth, or the visionary leader who empowers others to help build something greater than yourself. The choice—and the consequences—are yours.

The Emotional Journey of Delegation: Where Letting Go Powers Team Growth

Let's be real: delegation isn't just a logistical challenge – it's an emotional rollercoaster. You'll feel fear, uncertainty, maybe even a sense of loss. That's normal. In fact, if you don't feel a little uncomfortable, you're probably not delegating enough. And slowly it will diminish, and you will feel that "I am glad, I delegated".

But here's the beautiful part: on the other side of that discomfort is freedom. Freedom to focus on what truly matters. Freedom to grow your business in ways you never thought possible. Freedom to become the leader you're meant to be.

Remember: discomfort is the price of growth. Embrace it. Use it as a signpost that you're on the right track.

Conclusion: Your Delegation Revolution Starts Now

As we wrap up this chapter, I want you to imagine two versions of yourself a year from now. In one version, you're still trying to do it all, stretched thin, stressed out, and stagnating. In the other, you're leading a team of empowered individuals, focusing on high-level strategy, and watching your business soar to new heights.

Which version do you choose?

The power of delegation isn't just in what it allows you to offload – it's in what it allows you to become. It's about transforming yourself from a frazzled juggler into a visionary leader. It's about creating a business that can thrive with or without your constant involvement.

Ray Kroc didn't build McDonald's by flipping burgers. He built it by empowering others to flip burgers while he focused on the big picture. Now it's your turn. Your delegation revolution starts now. Are you ready?

Key Takeaways:

- Delegation is not just about tasks – it's about mindset and personal growth.
- Effective delegation multiplies your impact and scales your business.
- Embracing vulnerability in delegation opens up new possibilities.
- Delegation is an emotional journey – discomfort is normal and necessary.
- Not delegating is a choice to limit your own growth and your business's potential.

Final Action Step: Your Delegation Commitment

Write a letter to yourself, dated one year from now. Describe the business you've built through effective delegation. How has your role changed? How has your team grown? How do you feel as a leader? Make this vision so compelling that you can't help but take action to make it a reality.

Remember, the journey of delegation starts with a single task. What will you delegate today?

Chapter 17

Emotional Intelligence - Your Secret Weapon in Business

> What really matters for success, character, happiness and lifelong achievements is a definite set of emotional skills - your EQ - not just purely cognitive abilities that are measured by conventional IQ tests."
> - Daniel Goleman

Drawing from my experiences scaling multiple businesses, I reveal in this chapter why emotional intelligence is the hidden multiplier that sets great entrepreneurs apart from good ones. This chapter distills decades of hard-won insights into practical strategies for developing your EQ, showing you how understanding and managing emotions—both yours and others'—becomes your secret weapon for building stronger teams, deeper customer relationships, and ultimately, more successful businesses.

On a chilly February morning in 2014, Satya Nadella stepped into his new role as CEO of Microsoft, a tech giant that had lost its innovative edge. The company was struggling with internal competition, stagnant growth, and a reputation for arrogance. What happened next would become a masterclass in the power of emotional intelligence in business leadership.

Nadella's first act wasn't to announce a new product or restructure departments. Instead, he sent an email to every Microsoft employee, sharing his personal story of immigrating to the U.S. from India and his journey within the company. He spoke about his son's cerebral palsy and how it taught him empathy. He asked employees to rediscover their passion and purpose. This wasn't just a feel-good message. It was the beginning of a radical transformation, one that would see Microsoft's market value skyrocket from $300 billion to over $2 trillion in just seven years.

But here's the kicker: Nadella's approach wasn't some touchy-feely BS. It was a strategic application of emotional intelligence (EQ) that would revolutionize Microsoft's culture and business performance.

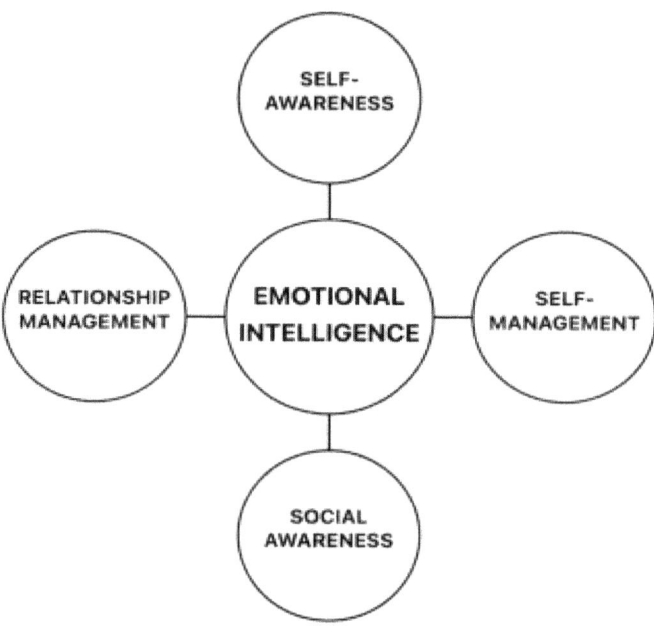

Chapter 17: Emotional Intelligence - Your Secret Weapon in Business

Now, I know what some of you are thinking. "Kay Kay, I'm in business to make money, not to get in touch with my feelings." But here's the truth bomb I'm about to drop on you: your EQ is just as crucial to your success as an entrepreneur as your IQ - maybe even more so.

Let me share a personal story that drives this home. In my early days in multifamily investing. Fresh from my success in gas stations, laundromats and single-family investments, I thought I could win in multifamily real estate with pure analytics and market research. I'd enter investor meetings armed with detailed financial models and perfect pitch decks yet struggled to convince the investors. What I failed to realize was that while numbers tell a story, people invest in people. The breakthrough came when I started sharing my immigrant entrepreneurship journey and my vision and how I built generational wealth through real estate investing.

It wasn't until I started focusing on developing my emotional intelligence that things really took off. I learned to read people's pain points, emotions, shared my own success story and manage my own reactions, and communicate in a way that resonated on an emotional level. Suddenly, I was building stronger relationships with my investors, closing more deals, and raising more capital for our deals more effectively.

Now, let's break down why emotional intelligence is so damn important for entrepreneurs:

1. It Boosts Your Decision-Making Skills: A study published in the Journal of Organizational Behavior found that leaders with high EQ make better decisions under pressure. Why? Because they're better at managing their own emotions and reading others', allowing them to stay calm and make rational choices even in high-stress situations.

Try this: Next time you're faced with a tough decision, take a moment to check in with your emotions. Are you feeling anxious? Excited? Overwhelmed? Recognizing these feelings can help you separate emotional reactions from logical thinking.

2. It Enhances Your Leadership Abilities: Research from the Center for Creative Leadership shows that 75% of careers are derailed for reasons related to emotional competencies, including inability to handle interpersonal problems, unsatisfactory team leadership during times of difficulty or conflict, or inability to adapt to change or elicit trust.

Challenge yourself: For the next week, make a conscious effort to really listen to your team members. Not just their words, but their tone, their body language, their unspoken concerns. Watch how this deeper understanding transforms your leadership.

3. It Improves Your Negotiation Skills: A study in the International Journal of Conflict Management found that negotiators with high EQ achieved better outcomes than their counterparts. They were better at reading the other party's emotions and adjusting their approach accordingly.

Make it a habit: Before your next negotiation, spend some time considering the other party's perspective. What might they be feeling? What are their underlying concerns? This empathy can help you find win-win solutions.

4. It Helps You Handle Stress Better: Entrepreneurship is a rollercoaster, and high EQ can be your seatbelt. Research published in Personality and Individual Differences shows that individuals with high EQ experience less stress and are better equipped to cope with it.

Practice this: Next time you're feeling stressed, try the 5-5-5 method. Name five things you can see, five things you can hear, and five things you can feel. This grounding exercise can help you regain emotional balance.

5. It Drives Innovation and Creativity: Contrary to the myth of the lone genius, innovation is a team sport. A study in the Journal of Product Innovation Management found that teams with higher average EQ were more innovative. Why? Because they were better at collaborating, handling conflicts, and building on each other's ideas.

Start small: In your next brainstorming session, focus not just on generating ideas, but on creating an emotionally safe space where team members feel comfortable sharing their thoughts, no matter how "out there" they might seem.

Now, I can hear some of you saying, "But Kay Kay, I'm just not a touchy-feely person. I can't change who I am." And I get it. Developing your EQ might feel uncomfortable at first, especially if you're used to focusing solely on logic and data. But here's the thing: emotional intelligence isn't about changing who you are. It's about expanding your capabilities and becoming a more well-rounded leader.

So how do you actually develop your emotional intelligence? Let's break it down into actionable steps:

6. Practice Self-Awareness: Start by tuning into your own emotions. Pause throughout the day and ask yourself: "What am I feeling right now? Why am I feeling this way?" This simple practice can dramatically increase your emotional self-awareness. Learn to notice the subtle shifts in your emotional landscape – the tension, the sense of accomplishment, the underlying anxiety. Understanding your emotional patterns is like learning to read a personal map, where each feeling points toward deeper self-knowledge.

This awareness is particularly valuable in challenging moments, as it allows you to recognize your emotional triggers before they overwhelm you. The practice isn't about judging these emotions but developing a compassionate understanding of your internal world and acknowledging that each feeling contributes to your complete experience.

7. Develop Empathy: Empathy is like a muscle - the more you use it, the stronger it becomes. Try this simple exercise to build your empathic capacity: Next time you find yourself in a conversation, shift your focus entirely away from your own agenda or what you're going to say next. Instead, make a conscious effort to truly listen and understand the other person's perspective. Put yourself in their shoes, imagining how the world looks from their vantage point. What emotions might they be

feeling? What experiences or concerns are shaping their point of view? Resist the urge to formulate your response while they are speaking. Instead, be fully present and attentive, allowing their words and nonverbal cues to paint a vivid picture of their internal experience.

8. Manage Your Emotions: Emotional management doesn't mean suppressing your feelings. It means acknowledging them and choosing how to respond constructively. When you feel a strong emotion arising, try the STOP technique:

When an intense feeling emerges, the first step is to stop what you're doing immediately - creating a crucial moment of disengagement that separates the emotion from your typical reactive pattern. Next, take a deep, intentional breath, inhaling slowly and fully before exhaling completely, allowing this conscious breathing to activate your parasympathetic nervous system and bring a sense of calm to both body and mind.

Then, become an impartial witness to your internal experience, observing your thoughts and feelings with curiosity and compassion rather than judgment - notice the physical sensations in your body, the racing thoughts in your mind, and identify the core emotion driving your impulse to act. Finally, with this newfound clarity and pause, proceed mindfully by consciously choosing how to respond - carefully consider whether there's a constructive way to express the emotion or if it's better to let it pass without immediate action, ensuring that whatever steps you take next are approached with intention and presence.

9. Improve Your Social Skills: Your social skills serve as the outward manifestation of your emotional intelligence, and developing these skills can have a transformative impact on your relationships. This development begins with practicing active listening - rather than planning your next response during conversations, focus on giving your full attention, maintaining eye contact, and paraphrasing to demonstrate genuine understanding and respect. Equally important is the art of graceful feedback exchange: provide constructive input with empathy to foster

Chapter 17: Emotional Intelligence - Your Secret Weapon in Business

others' growth, while receiving feedback non-defensively as an opportunity for self-awareness and improvement.

When it comes to conflict resolution, remember that while disagreements are natural, your approach to handling them is crucial - avoid escalation by actively seeking to understand opposing perspectives, identifying common ground, and working toward solutions that benefit all parties. While mastering these social skills requires sustained dedication and patience, the rewards are substantial: you'll forge stronger relationships, expand your sphere of influence, and evolve into a more effective communicator. Remember to approach this journey with patience, viewing each interaction as an opportunity to enhance your interpersonal capabilities.

10. Seek Feedback: To enhance your emotional intelligence, actively seek honest feedback from trusted colleagues and mentors, as their external perspectives can illuminate blind spots you might not recognize on your own. Don't hesitate to ask specific questions about areas where they see potential for growth and encourage them to share observations about your behavioral patterns and tendencies, making sure to receive their insights with gratitude rather than defensiveness.

Make your feedback requests concrete and actionable by asking about specific situations - for instance, inquiring whether you appeared impatient during a recent meeting - as these tangible examples provide clear areas for improvement. While receiving feedback can be challenging, view it as a valuable gift that offers opportunities for deeper self-awareness and emotional skill development, approaching it with an open mindset that integrates external perspectives with your own self-reflection. Remember that consistently seeking feedback is a clear indicator of a growth mindset and demonstrates your commitment to ongoing self-improvement - it's a characteristic that distinguishes emotionally intelligent individuals who understand that learning is a continuous journey.

Remember, developing your EQ is a journey, not a destination. It takes time and consistent effort, but the payoff is enormous.

Now, let's talk about vulnerability. I know, I know. The word alone probably makes some of you uncomfortable. But hear me out. Vulnerability isn't weakness. In fact, it's one of the most powerful tools in a leader's arsenal.

When I first started sharing my own struggles and uncertainties with my team, I was terrified. I thought they'd lose respect for me. But you know what happened? They opened up too. Our relationships deepened. Trust skyrocketed. And suddenly, we were solving problems and innovating in ways we never had before.

Research backs this up. A study by the Harvard Business Review found that leaders who were willing to show vulnerability - admitting mistakes, asking for help, sharing doubts - were seen as more authentic and trustworthy by their teams.

So, here's your challenge: This week, share something vulnerable with your team. It could be a mistake you made, a fear you have, or a time you felt out of your depth. Watch how this act of authenticity transforms your relationships and your team's performance.

Now, let's get real for a second. Developing your EQ isn't always going to be comfortable. There will be times when you'd rather go back to focusing solely on numbers and strategy. But remember why you're doing this. Remember the improved relationships, the enhanced leadership skills, and the overall success that await on the other side of improved emotional intelligence.

Here's a powerful truth I want you to internalize: Your EQ is not fixed. No matter where you're starting from, you can improve your emotional intelligence. And as you do, you'll see improvements in every area of your business and life.

Chapter 17: Emotional Intelligence - Your Secret Weapon in Business

So, I challenge you: For the next 30 days, commit to one EQ-building activity each day. It could be as simple as taking five minutes to reflect on your emotions, or as challenging as having a difficult conversation you've been avoiding.

Will it be comfortable? Not always. Will there be times when you'd rather go back to focusing solely on logic and data? Absolutely. But remember why you're doing this. Remember the improved relationships, the enhanced leadership skills, and the overall success that await on the other side of improved emotional intelligence.

You have the power to develop your EQ and become a more effective, empathetic, and successful entrepreneur. You have the ability to not just understand business, but to understand people - including yourself. And in doing so, you'll not only build a more successful business - but you'll also become a more fulfilled, well-rounded human being.

So, are you ready to boost your EQ? Are you ready to unlock this secret weapon for business success? The choice is yours. And I believe in you.

Let's develop that emotional intelligence. Let's become leaders who understand not just strategies and numbers, but people and emotions. Your next level of success is waiting on the other side of your improved EQ. Go seize it.

Action Steps:

1. Take an EQ assessment to establish your baseline. There are many free online options available or use the tool to take the assessment at the end of this chapter.
2. Based on your assessment results, create a personal development plan. Identify your weakest EQ area and set specific goals to improve it over the next month.
3. Start an "Emotion Journal". For the next week, take 5 minutes each evening to write down the emotions you experienced that day and what triggered them.
4. Practice the "Name it to tame it" technique. When you feel a strong emotion, simply naming it can help you manage it better. Try this throughout your day.
5. Set up a "Feedback Circle" with trusted accountability partner, colleagues or mentors. Meet regularly to give and receive honest feedback on your emotional intelligence and leadership skills.

Remember, developing your emotional intelligence isn't about becoming someone you're not. It's about becoming the best version of yourself. It's about unlocking capabilities you already have within you. Your journey to higher EQ starts now. Let's make it count.

Key Takeaways:

- Emotional Intelligence (EQ) is crucial for entrepreneurial success, impacting decision-making, leadership, negotiation, stress management, and innovation.
- EQ can be developed through practices like self-awareness, empathy, emotion management, and improved social skills.
- Vulnerability in leadership can lead to increased trust and better team performance.
- Your EQ is not fixed - with consistent effort, you can improve your emotional intelligence and see benefits across all areas of your business and life.

Chapter 17: Emotional Intelligence - Your Secret Weapon in Business

Emotional Intelligence (EQ) Assessment Tool:

Instructions: Rate yourself on a scale of 1-5 for each statement below:

1 = Never/Rarely
2 = Sometimes
3 = Often
4 = Very Often
5 = Almost Always

Part 1: Self-Awareness

1. I can accurately identify my emotions as I experience them. ____
2. I understand how my emotions affect my behavior. ____
3. I recognize my emotional triggers. ____
4. I'm aware of my strengths and limitations. ____
5. I can tell when my emotions are influencing my decisions. ____
6. I know when I need to take a step back and reflect. ____
7. I understand how others' actions affect my emotional state. ____
8. I can identify when I'm experiencing stress or pressure. ____

Score: ____ /40

Less than 20: Developing Self-Awareness
21-30: Moderate Self-Awareness
31-40: Strong Self-Awareness

Part 2: Self-Management

1. I can stay composed under pressure. ____
2. I adapt well to changing situations. ____

3. I can control impulsive feelings and behaviors. ____
4. I follow through on commitments. ____
5. I take initiative when needed. ____
6. I can pause before acting on emotions. ____
7. I maintain focus despite emotional distractions. ____
8. I can bounce back from setbacks. ____

Score: ____ /40

Less than 20: Developing Self-Management
21-30: Moderate Self-Management
31-40: Strong Self-Management

Part 3: Social Awareness

1. I can accurately read others' emotions. ____
2. I pick up on nonverbal cues. ____
3. I understand others' perspectives, even when I disagree. ____
4. I'm aware of group dynamics and power relationships. ____
5. I can sense when someone is upset, even if they don't say it. ____
6. I understand cultural differences in emotional expression. ____
7. I recognize when others need support. ____
8. I can tell when a group's mood is shifting. ____

Score: ____ /40

Less than 20: Developing Social Awareness
21-30: Moderate Social Awareness
31-40: Strong Social Awareness

Part 4: Relationship Management

1. I communicate clearly and effectively. ____
2. I can handle difficult conversations constructively. ____
3. I build and maintain strong relationships. ____
4. I can resolve conflicts effectively. ____
5. I give constructive feedback. ____
6. I inspire and influence others positively. ____
7. I work well in teams. ____
8. I help others develop and grow. ____

Score: ____ /40

Chapter 17: Emotional Intelligence - Your Secret Weapon in Business

Less than 20: Developing Relationship Management
21-30: Moderate Relationship Management
31-40: Strong Relationship Management

Part 5: Emotional Reasoning

1. I consider emotions when making decisions. ____
2. I can balance logic and feelings. ____
3. I understand how emotions affect judgment. ____
4. I use emotional information to solve problems. ____
5. I can identify the root causes of emotions. ____
6. I consider multiple perspectives when problem-solving. ____
7. I make decisions that account for both short and long-term emotions. ____
8. I can evaluate the emotional impact of my choices

Score: ____ /40

Less than 20: Developing Emotional Reasoning
21-30: Moderate Emotional Reasoning
31-40: Strong Emotional Reasoning

Scoring and Interpretation

Total Score: ____ /200

Overall EQ Level:

- 0-80: Developing EQ - Focus on building foundational emotional awareness and skills
- 81-140: Moderate EQ - Continue strengthening emotional competencies
- 141-180: Strong EQ - Refine and apply advanced emotional intelligence skills
- 181-200: Exceptional EQ - Maintain and share your emotional intelligence expertise

Profile Analysis

For each section where you scored:

- Less than 20: This is an area for focused development
- 21-30: This is an area of moderate strength with room for growth
- 31-40: This is an area of significant strength

Development Plan

1. Identify your lowest-scoring area: _____
2. Set three specific goals for improvement in this area:

   - Goal 1: _____
   - Goal 2: _____
   - Goal 3: _____

3. Action steps to achieve these goals:

   - Daily practice: _____
   - Weekly practice: _____
   - Monthly review: _____

Regular Assessment

Schedule to retake this assessment:

- Date of this assessment: _____
- Next assessment date (3 months): _____
- Six-month review date: _____

Remember:

- EQ can be developed with practice and dedication
- Focus on one area of improvement at a time
- Seek feedback from others on your progress
- Be patient with yourself as you develop these skills
- Regular self-reflection is key to EQ development

Additional Notes

Use this space to record insights, patterns, or specific situations where you notice your EQ affecting your interactions:

Date completed: _____

Chapter 18

The Persistence Principle - Never Give Up, Never Surrender

> Many of life's failures are people who did not realize how close they were to success when they gave up."
> - Thomas Edison

Drawing from my journey as an immigrant entrepreneur who built multiple successful businesses, I'll show you why persistence is the ultimate differentiator between those who dream and those who achieve. This chapter reveals battle-tested strategies for developing unwavering persistence, demonstrating how to transform setbacks into steppingstones and self-doubt into unstoppable determination.

In 1978, a young British engineer named James Dyson became frustrated with his Hoover vacuum cleaner. The bag kept clogging, reducing suction and leaving his carpets dirty. Instead of complaining or buying a new vacuum, Dyson did something that would change the course of his life - and the cleaning industry forever.

He decided to build a better vacuum: What followed was a grueling 15-year odyssey of trial and error. Dyson built prototype after prototype, each one failing in new and interesting ways. His savings dwindled. His wife supported the family by teaching art classes. Friends and family thought he was crazy.

But Dyson persisted: He didn't just fail once or twice. He failed 5,126 times. That's right - 5,126 prototypes that didn't work. But with each failure, he learned something new. He refined his design, tweaked his approach, and kept pushing forward.

Finally, on prototype number 5,127, it worked. The world's first bagless vacuum cleaner was born.

Today, Dyson is a household name, with a net worth of over $9 billion. But here's the kicker: if he had given up on prototype 5,000, or even 5,100, we might never have heard of him.

Now, I know what some of you are thinking. "That's a cool story, Kay Kay, but what does it have to do with me? I'm not trying to invent a vacuum cleaner." Fair enough. But here's the truth bomb I'm about to drop on you: Persistence isn't just for inventors. It's the secret sauce of every successful entrepreneur. It's what separates the dreamers from the doers, the wishers from the achievers.

Let me share a personal story. When I first ventured into multifamily investing, I knew social media would be crucial for success. I started posting daily on Instagram, going live on Facebook, and even being a guest on real estate podcasts. There were weeks where I'd spend countless hours crafting the perfect content - sharing market insights, investment strategies, and property transformation stories - only to get a handful of likes and zero engagement. I'd refresh my analytics obsessively, watching those dismal numbers mock my efforts. The silence was deafening. Here I was, sharing valuable knowledge from years of experience, and it felt like I was speaking into a void.

But instead of letting the algorithms defeat me, I chose to pivot and persist. I created a Facebook Group called "10X Multifamily Investment Group," focusing on building a community rather than just broadcasting content. I showed up every day, answering questions, sharing wins and losses, and providing real value through live training sessions on zoom calls. Most importantly, I stayed authentic - sharing not just the glossy success stories, but the hard lessons and challenges too. And you know what? The community responded. Slowly but surely, the group grew from a few hundred members to thousands of engaged members and investors. Today, our community has become a thriving ecosystem of like-minded real estate entrepreneurs, with thousands of members across Facebook. I've helped countless people start their real estate journey, but perhaps more importantly, it's transformed my own approach to business and leadership.

That's the Power of Persistence: Where Small Steps Write Epic Stories

Numerous studies have shed light on the powerful role that persistence plays in entrepreneurial success. A landmark study published in the Journal of Personality and Social Psychology found that "grit" - a combination of deep passion and unwavering perseverance - is an even better predictor of achievement than raw intelligence or natural talent. In other words, it's not just about how smart you are or how gifted you may be; it's about how long you're willing to stick with your goals, even in the face of obstacles and setbacks.

Building on this research, a study from the University of Pennsylvania revealed that entrepreneurs who exhibited high levels of grit were far more likely to maintain the operational viability of their businesses over time. These gritty founders were also more inclined to pursue ambitious growth strategies and drive continuous innovation - a critical competitive advantage - rather than succumbing to the inevitable challenges that arise.

But the story gets even more fascinating when you consider the psychological mechanisms underlying persistence. Recent research from the University of Southern California suggests that an entrepreneur's capacity for persistence is not solely dependent on raw willpower or determination. Rather, it is deeply influenced by their underlying mindset and the way they interpret and respond to setbacks.

Entrepreneurs with a "growth mindset" - those who view challenges not as threats, but as opportunities for learning and improvement - tend to display far greater levels of persistence than their peers. When faced with obstacles, these individuals can reframe the experience, seeing it as a chance to develop new skills, refine their strategies, and ultimately emerge stronger. In contrast, entrepreneurs with a more fixed mindset are more likely to be derailed by failures and disappointments, interpreting them as reflections of their inherent limitations.

This distinction highlights a crucial point: Persistence is not just about brute force or an unbreakable will; it is also about cultivating a resilient, adaptable, and opportunity-oriented mindset. By developing this cognitive flexibility, entrepreneurs can transform potential pitfalls into launching pads for growth, innovation, and sustained success.

Ultimately, the research is clear: For entrepreneurs seeking to navigate the unpredictable and often tumultuous journey of building a business, persistence - grounded in a growth mindset - is not just a desirable trait, but a strategic imperative. It is the wellspring from which the greatest entrepreneurial triumphs emerge.

So, why is persistence so crucial for entrepreneurs? Let's break it down:

1. It Overcomes Obstacles: In business, obstacles are inevitable. Persistence is what helps you find a way around, over, or through those obstacles.

Try this: Next time you face a setback, instead of getting discouraged, ask yourself, "What's one small step I can take to move forward?" Then take that step, no matter how small.

2. It Builds Resilience: The more you persist through tough times, the more resilient you become. This resilience is like a superpower in the entrepreneurial world.

Challenge yourself: For the next 30 days, commit to taking action towards your goals every single day, no matter how you feel. Watch how this builds your resilience muscle.

3. It Leads to Innovation: When you persist in the face of challenges, you're often forced to think creatively and find new solutions. This is where innovation happens.

Make it a habit: When faced with a problem, challenge yourself to come up with at least three possible solutions before giving up.

4. It Attracts Success: Persistence is magnetic. It attracts opportunities, resources, and people who can help you succeed.

Practice this: Start sharing your journey - both the ups and downs - on social media or with your network that is open declaration. You'll be surprised at the support and opportunities that come your way when people see your commitment.

5. It Builds Character: Persistence doesn't just help you achieve your goals - it shapes who you are as a person and an entrepreneur.

Start small: Choose one small goal and commit to working towards it every day for a month, no matter what. Notice how this commitment shapes your character.

Now, I can hear some of you saying, "But Kay Kay, what if I've been persisting and nothing's working? When do I know it's time to quit?" And that's a valid question. Persistence isn't about stubbornly sticking to a failing strategy. It's about staying committed to your vision while being flexible in your approach.

This is where the concept of pivoting comes in. A pivot isn't giving up - it's a course correction. It's saying, "This specific approach isn't working, but I'm still committed to solving this problem or achieving this goal."

Take the story of Slack, the popular workplace communication tool. It didn't start as Slack. It started as a video game called Glitch. When the game failed to gain traction, instead of giving up, the team pivoted. They took a small feature of the game - the chat function - and turned it into a standalone product. That product became Slack, which was sold to Salesforce for $27.7 billion in 2021.

That's the power of combining persistence with flexibility. You stay committed to your overall vision, but you're willing to change your approach based on feedback and results. Let us break it down in the following steeps.

1.Set Clear, Compelling Goals: Having a clear, inspiring vision of what you're working towards provides a powerful source of motivation when the road gets tough. Defining specific, measurable goals gives you a tangible target to strive for, rather than a vague notion of success. Regularly revisiting and refining these goals can help you stay laser-focused and energized, even in the face of obstacles.

2.Break Big Goals into Smaller Steps: Ambitious, long-term goals can feel daunting and overwhelming, making it easy to get discouraged along the way. By breaking these big objectives down into more manageable, incremental steps, you create a sense of progress and frequent opportunities for small wins. This steady cadence of achievement helps sustain your motivation and persistence over the long haul.

3.Develop a Growth Mindset: Your interpretation of setbacks and challenges is a key determinant of your ability to persist. Entrepreneurs with a "growth mindset" - those who view obstacles as chances to learn and improve, rather than as reflections of their inherent limitations - consistently demonstrate

Chapter 18: The Persistence Principle - Never Give Up, Never Surrender

greater resilience. By reframing failures as valuable feedback, you can stay open, adaptable, and empowered to push forward.

4. Build a Support Network: Entrepreneurship can be an isolating journey, making it critical to surround yourself with people who believe in you and your vision. Trusted mentors, encouraging friends, and like-minded peers can provide the moral support, strategic advice, and practical assistance you need to stay motivated and overcome hurdles. Tapping into this network can be a powerful antidote to loneliness and self-doubt.

5. Practice Self-Care: Persistence requires sustained energy, focus, and mental clarity. By making your physical and emotional well-being a priority through practices like exercise, healthy eating, and stress management, you ensure that you have the necessary resources to keep pushing forward, even when the going gets tough. Burnout is the enemy of persistence, so investing in self-care is an essential strategy.

6. Celebrate Small Wins: In the midst of a long, grueling journey, it's easy to lose sight of your progress and get discouraged. That's why it's so important to regularly acknowledge and celebrate even the smallest steps forward. These "mini milestones" reinforce your sense of momentum and achievement, fueling your motivation to persist through the next challenge.

7. Learn from Setbacks: Failure and disappointment are inevitable on the entrepreneurial path, but your response to these setbacks is what truly matters. Rather than letting them derail you, approach each challenge as an opportunity to gather valuable insights and refine your strategies. By cultivating this growth-oriented mindset, you transform obstacles into catalysts for improvement and continued progress.

8. Visualize Success: The power of visualization should not be underestimated. By regularly picturing yourself achieving your goals - whether it's closing a big deal, launching a new product, or hitting a crucial revenue target - you activate the neural pathways associated with those outcomes. This cognitive rehearsal can

bolster your confidence and resilience, helping you persevere even when the path ahead seems uncertain.

9.Develop a 'Why' That's Bigger Than You: When your entrepreneurial journey is fueled by a sense of purpose that extends beyond your own personal success, it becomes easier to maintain your persistence through challenging times. Whether it's a desire to solve a pressing social problem, create more economic opportunities in your community, or leave a legacy, tapping into a larger "why" can imbue your work with a deeper sense of meaning and significance.

10.Practice Patience: Entrepreneurial success rarely happens overnight. It's a long, winding, and often unpredictable journey that requires an unwavering commitment to the process. Embracing patience and refusing to be deterred by the natural ebb and flow of progress is a hallmark of the most persistent founders. Trusting the journey, even when the path is unclear, can help you stay the course and ultimately achieve your vision.

Now, let's talk about vulnerability. I know, I know. The word alone probably makes some of you uncomfortable. But hear me out. Vulnerability isn't weakness. In fact, it's a crucial component of persistence.

Let me share a personal story, about a critical turning point from my ground-up gas station development. Despite my experience operating multiple successful stations, this new venture was bleeding money every month, even with its modern facilities. Instead of hiding behind the typical entrepreneur's mask of "everything's fine," I chose vulnerability. I openly shared our struggles with partners and fellow operators—the cash flow challenges, sleepless nights over fuel pricing, and doubts about choosing new construction over acquiring an existing station. This honesty, though difficult, proved transformative. What I feared would damage my reputation actually strengthened my business relationships and led to invaluable insights from others who had faced similar challenges.

Chapter 18: The Persistence Principle - Never Give Up, Never Surrender

And you know, the result was transformative. My vulnerability sparked an unexpected wave of support from fellow operators who began sharing their own challenges and solutions. Competitors became collaborators—routing diesel customers our way, offering layout advice, and sharing pricing strategies. What I feared would be seen as weakness became my strength, building a network of industry allies invested in our success. This experience fundamentally changed my approach to business.

Research backs this up. A study by the Harvard Business Review found that leaders who were willing to show vulnerability - admitting mistakes, sharing doubts, asking for help - were seen as more authentic and trustworthy by their teams.

So, here's your challenge: This week, share a struggle you're facing in your business journey. It could be with your team, your audience, partner or even just a trusted friend. Watch how this act of vulnerability strengthens your relationships and support network.

Remember, persistence isn't about never feeling discouraged or wanting to quit. It's about feeling those things and choosing to keep going anyway.

Here's a powerful truth I want you to internalize: Your persistence is directly linked to your success as an entrepreneur. It's not about who has the best idea or the most resources - it's about who's willing to stick with it the longest.

So, I challenge you: For the next 30 days, commit to taking action towards your goals every single day, no matter how small. Even on the days when you don't feel like it. Especially on the days when you don't feel like it.

Will it be easy? No. Will there be days when you want to throw in the towel? Absolutely. But remember why you're doing this. Remember the dreams, the impact, and the success that await on the other side of persistence.

You have the power to turn your entrepreneurial dreams into reality. You have the ability to overcome any obstacle that stands in your way. And in persisting, you'll not only build a successful business - but you'll also become a stronger, more resilient person.

So, are you ready to embrace the power of persistence? Are you ready to commit to never giving up on your dreams? The choice is yours. And I believe in you.

Let's persist. Let's keep pushing forward, one step at a time. Your success is waiting on the other side of your persistence. Go seize it.

Action Steps:

1. Create a "Persistence Plan" for your most challenging current goal. Break it down into small, daily actions you can take over the next 30 days.
2. Start a "Persistence Journal". Each day, write down one action you took towards your goal and one obstacle you overcame.
3. Identify your "Why". Write a mission statement that goes beyond personal success. Why does your goal matter? Who will it help?
4. Create a "Failure Resume". List your biggest setbacks and what you learned from each. Review it when you need a reminder of your resilience.
5. Schedule a "Vulnerability Share". This week, share a current struggle with someone you trust. Notice how it affects your relationship and motivation.

Key Takeaways:

- Persistence is a key predictor of entrepreneurial success, more important than natural talent or IQ.
- Persistence isn't just about willpower - it's about how you interpret and learn from setbacks.
- Effective persistence involves staying committed to your vision while being flexible in your approach.
- Vulnerability can strengthen persistence by building authentic connections and support networks.
- Persistence is a skill that can be developed through consistent practice and the right mindset.

Remember, persistence isn't about never falling down - it's about getting back up every single time you fall. Your journey to unshakeable persistence starts now. Let's make it count.

Chapter 19

The Ethics Advantage - Building a Business with Integrity

> In looking for people to hire, look for three qualities: integrity, intelligence, and energy. And if they don't have the first, the other two will kill you."
> - Warren Buffett

Through decades of business experience, I've discovered that building a business with integrity isn't just the right thing to do—it's the smart thing to do. This chapter reveals how ethical business practices become your greatest competitive advantage, sharing proven strategies for creating lasting success while making decisions you can be proud of.

On a crisp autumn day in 1973, a young climber and surfer named Yvon Chouinard made a decision that would revolutionize the outdoor industry and challenge the very foundations of business ethics. Chouinard, the founder of Patagonia, discovered that the steel pitons his company produced were damaging the rock faces of Yosemite National Park. Despite these pitons being his main source of revenue, he made the radical choice to phase them out entirely.

This wasn't just a product decision. It was a declaration of values that would shape Patagonia's entire business model for decades to come. Chouinard chose environmental responsibility over profit, authenticity over convenience, long-term sustainability over short-term gains.

Fast forward to today, and Patagonia is a billion-dollar company with a cult-like following. But here's the kicker: they've achieved this success not despite their ethical stance, but because of it.

Now, I know what some of you are thinking. "Come on, Kay Kay. That's a nice story, but in the real world, you've got to be cutthroat to succeed. Nice guys finish last, right?"

Wrong. Dead wrong. And I'm about to drop some truth bombs that will blow that outdated myth right out of the water.

The Ethics Revolution

We're living in an era where business ethics isn't just a nice-to-have—it's a critical competitive advantage. The numbers tell a compelling story: companies with strong ethical practices outperform their peers by 33% in customer loyalty, 38% in employee retention, and 27% in market valuation. But beyond the statistics lies a deeper truth: ethical business practices are reshaping the very nature of entrepreneurial success.

Think about this: 76% of consumers would switch brands to one that better aligns with their values, even if it costs more. The message is clear ethics isn't just good karma; it's good business.

The ROI of Ethical Leadership

Let me share something controversial: ethical business practices often cost more in the short term. They require more time, more resources, and more commitment. But here's what I've learned from building and scaling multiple businesses: the long-term returns are exponentially higher as compared to short term returns.

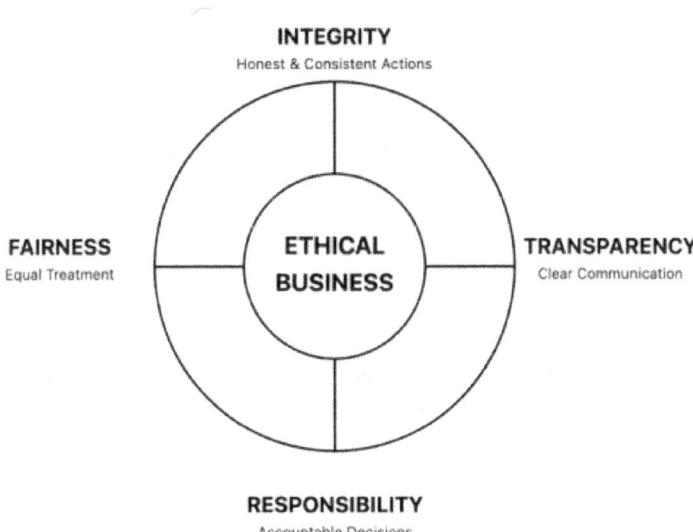

Business Ethics Framework

Let me share a personal story from my early business career. As a Gas Station & convenience store owner, I faced a challenging ethical decision. A new product called K2, technically legal but essentially a synthetic drug, was generating massive profits for gas stations across the region. When my partners asked me to stock it, given its exceptional sales potential, I stood firm in my principle: if I wouldn't sell something to my own children, I won't sell it to others' children. My instincts proved right – the product's marketing claims were misleading, and authorities eventually banned it completely. This decision, while costly in the short term, reinforced my commitment to ethical business practices.

While others might have rationalized it as a standard business decision, my conscience wouldn't allow it. Despite the clear financial implications - reduced profits and slower business expansion - I declined the opportunity. The choice reflected a deeper commitment to values over immediate financial gain.

You know what happened? Word got out about my decision. People started to trust me more. Clients who valued integrity sought me out. In the long run, that one ethical decision paid off far more than any short-term gain ever could have.

But don't just take my word for it. Let's look at the cold, hard facts.

A study published in the Journal of Business Ethics found that companies with strong ethical cultures outperform their peers by almost 40% in terms of productivity, customer satisfaction, and employee retention. Another study by Ethisphere showed that the World's Most Ethical Companies outperformed the US Large Cap Index by 10.5% over a three-year period.

In other words, ethics isn't just a feel-good bonus. It's a powerful competitive advantage. So why is ethical business so crucial for entrepreneurs? Let's break it down:

1. It Builds Trust: In an age of information overload and fake news, trust is the most valuable currency. Ethical businesses build deep, lasting relationships with customers, employees, and partners.

Try this: List three ways you can increase transparency in your business this week. Maybe it's being more open about your pricing structure or sharing behind-the-scenes content of your work process.

2. It Attracts and Retains Top Talent: The best employees want to work for companies that align with their values. A

study by Deloitte found that 70% of millennials say a company's commitment to the community influences their decision to work there.

Challenge yourself: Create an "ethics statement" for your company. Share it with your team and ask for their input. Watch how this engages and motivates them.

3. It Mitigates Risk: Ethical companies are less likely to face scandals, lawsuits, or regulatory issues. This stability is attractive to investors and partners.

Make it a habit: Before making any significant business decision, ask yourself, "Would I be comfortable if this decision was on the front page of the newspaper?" If the answer is no, reconsider.

4. It Drives Innovation: Ethical constraints can actually spark creativity. When you're committed to doing the right thing, you're forced to think outside the box to solve problems.

Practice this: Next time you face a business challenge, brainstorm solutions that not only solve the problem but also create positive impact. You might be surprised at the innovative ideas that emerge.

5. It Creates Long-Term Sustainability: Ethical businesses think beyond quarterly profits. They build sustainable models that can weather economic storms and shifting market trends.

Start small: Identify one area where your business could be more sustainable. It could be reducing waste, improving energy efficiency, or implementing fair labor practices.

Now, I can hear some of you saying, "But Kay Kay, ethical decisions aren't always black and white. How do I navigate the gray areas?"

And you're right. Ethical dilemmas in business can be complex. But that's where having a strong ethical framework comes in handy. Here's a simple model you can use:

1. Identify the Ethical Issue: What's at stake? Who could be affected by your decision?

2. Gather Information: What are the facts? What are the potential consequences of different actions?

3. Consider Your Options: What are all the possible courses of action?

4. Evaluate Using Ethical Principles: Consider principles like fairness, harm prevention, respect for autonomy, and the greater good.

5. Make a Decision and Implement: Choose the option that best aligns with your ethical principles and implement it.

6. Reflect and Learn: After the decision, reflect on the outcomes. What did you learn? How can you apply this in the future?

Remember, being ethical doesn't mean being perfect. It means being committed to doing the right thing, even when it's hard. It means being willing to learn and grow from your mistakes.

Now, let's talk about vulnerability. I know, I know. The word alone probably makes some of you uncomfortable. But hear me out. Vulnerability isn't weakness. In fact, it's a crucial component of ethical leadership.

When I made the decision to turn down that unethical product, I was scared about missing the opportunity. I worried about how it would affect my business. I even questioned if I was being naive. But I chose to be vulnerable and share my decision-making process with my team and my partners.

Research backs this up. A study published in the Journal of Business Ethics found that leaders who demonstrate vulnerability - by admitting mistakes, sharing doubts, and asking for help - are perceived as more ethical and trustworthy by their teams.

So, here's your challenge: This week, share an ethical dilemma you're facing with your team, partners or a trusted advisor. Be open about your thought process and your doubts. Watch how this vulnerability strengthens your relationships and leads to better decisions.

Now, let's get real for a second. Building an ethical business isn't always going to be comfortable. There will be times when you'll be tempted to take shortcuts or look the other way. But remember why you're doing this. Remember the trust, the loyalty, and the long-term success that await on the other side of ethical decision-making.

Here's a powerful truth I want you to internalize: Your ethics are your brand. In a world where consumers are increasingly values-driven, your commitment to integrity can be your greatest differentiator.

So, I challenge you: For the next 30 days, commit to making one explicitly ethical decision each day in your business. It could be as simple as being more transparent in your marketing, or as significant as rethinking a supply chain to be more sustainable.

Will it be easy? Not always. Will there be times when you're tempted to compromise? Absolutely. But remember why you're doing this. Remember the impact you want to have, the legacy you want to leave.

You have the power to build a business that not only succeeds but makes the world a better place. You have the ability to lead with integrity and inspire others to do the same. And in doing so, you'll not only build a more successful business - but you'll also become a more fulfilled, impactful entrepreneur.

So, are you ready to embrace the ethics advantage? Are you ready to build a business with integrity at its core? The choice is yours. And I believe in you.

Let's build businesses that we can be proud of. Let's create success that goes beyond the bottom line. Your ethical advantage is waiting to be unleashed. Go seize it.

Action Steps:

1. Develop a Personal and Business Code of Ethics: Write down your core values and how they translate into business practices.
2. Conduct an Ethical Audit: Review your current business practices. Are there any areas where you could be more ethical or transparent?
3. Create an Ethics Discussion Group: Start a monthly meeting with your team to discuss ethical dilemmas and best practices.
4. Implement an Anonymous Feedback System: Give employees and customers a way to report ethical concerns without fear of reprisal.
5. Set Ethical Goals: Alongside your business goals, set specific ethical targets for the next quarter (e.g., reduce waste by 20%, implement a fair wage policy).

Key Takeaways:

- Ethical business practices lead to better long-term performance and sustainability.
- Having a strong ethical framework helps navigate complex business decisions.
- Vulnerability and transparency in ethical decision-making build trust and respect.
- Your commitment to ethics can be a powerful brand differentiator in a values-driven market.
- Building an ethical business is an ongoing process that requires consistent commitment and reflection.

Remember, building an ethical business isn't a one-time event. It's an ongoing commitment to doing the right thing, even when it's challenging. Your journey to becoming an ethical business leader starts now. Let's make it count.

Chapter 20

Your Entrepreneurial Odyssey - Putting It All Together

> The future belongs to those who believe in the beauty of their dreams."
> - Eleanor Roosevelt

In this final chapter, I bring together all the essential principles we've explored, showing you how to weave them into your own unique entrepreneurial journey. Drawing from three decades of business experience across multiple industries, I provide a practical roadmap for implementing these strategies, demonstrating how to transform the lessons learned throughout this book into concrete actions that will revolutionize your business and life.

In the summer of 1994, a young computer programmer named Jeff Bezos sat in his garage in Bellevue, Washington, surrounded by boxes and packing tape. He had just quit his high-paying job on Wall Street to pursue a wild idea: selling books online. Most people thought he was crazy. The internet was still new, and the idea of buying things online seemed far-fetched at best.

But Bezos wasn't just chasing a business idea. He was embarking on an entrepreneurial odyssey that would change the face of retail forever.

Fast forward to today, and Amazon is one of the most valuable companies in the world, revolutionizing not just book sales, but how we shop for everything. Bezos himself has become one of the wealthiest individuals on the planet.

Now, I know what you're thinking. "Great story, Kay Kay, but I'm not trying to be the next Jeff Bezos." And that's okay. Your entrepreneurial journey doesn't have to end with world domination (unless that's your thing, in which case, go for it). But here's the kicker: whether you're aiming to build a global empire or a thriving local business, the principles of entrepreneurial success are the same.

Throughout this book, we've explored these principles in depth. We've delved into the power of mindset, the importance of resilience, the art of innovation, and so much more. Now, it's time to put it all together and chart your own entrepreneurial odyssey.

But before we do that, let me share a personal story that brings home why this matters so much.

My entrepreneurial journey began thirty-five years ago in India, fresh out of college and brimming with ambition. Despite working tirelessly in our family farm, my scattered approach held me back. I had abundant creativity but lacked strategic direction. Like many young entrepreneurs, I struggled to channel my enthusiasm into focused action. My early attempts serve as a perfect example of misguided entrepreneurial energy.

Chapter 20: Your Entrepreneurial Odyssey - Putting It All Together

It wasn't until I started intentionally developing my entrepreneurial mindset - applying the very principles we've discussed in this book - that thing began to change. I learned to focus my energy, to persist through challenges, to innovate creatively, to lead with emotional intelligence, and to build a business with integrity.

The result? Not only did my travel agency business start to thrive, but I found a sense of fulfillment and purpose I'd never experienced before. I wasn't just building a business; I was growing as a person and making a positive impact on the world.

And here's the thing: if I can do it, so can you. But it starts with understanding and applying the key principles we've covered. So, let's recap:

1. The Power of Mindset: We learned that success starts in your mind. Your beliefs shape your reality. Remember Carol Dweck's research on the growth mindset? Entrepreneurs who believe their abilities can be developed through dedication and hard work are more likely to succeed than those who believe their talents are fixed traits.

2. Embracing Failure: We discovered that failure isn't the opposite of success - it's a crucial part of the journey. James Dyson's 5,126 failed prototypes before creating his revolutionary vacuum cleaner is a testament to this.

3. The Importance of Vision: We explored how having a clear, compelling vision can guide you through tough times. Elon Musk's vision of sustainable energy and space exploration has driven him to achieve the seemingly impossible.

4. Building Resilience: We learned strategies for bouncing back from setbacks and staying strong in the face of challenges. Angela Duckworth's research on grit showed us that perseverance is more important than talent in predicting success.

5. The Growth Mindset: We discovered the power of believing in your ability to learn and grow. This mindset is what allowed Sara Blakely to go from selling fax machines door-to-door to becoming the youngest self-made female billionaire with Spanx.

6. Effective Time Management: We explored techniques for making the most of your time and energy. Remember, you have the same 24 hours in a day as anyone else - it's how you use them that counts.

7. The Art of Networking: We learned how to build meaningful connections that can propel your business forward. As Reid Hoffman, co-founder of LinkedIn, says, "Your network is your net worth."

8. Financial Intelligence: We discovered the importance of understanding and managing your finances. Warren Buffett didn't become one of the world's wealthiest individuals by chance - he mastered the art of financial management.

9. Innovation and Creativity: We explored ways to think outside the box and bring fresh ideas to your business. Steve Jobs' ability to see connections between seemingly unrelated fields led to groundbreaking innovations at Apple.

10. The Confidence Factor: We learned how to build unshakeable confidence in yourself and your abilities. As Henry Ford said, "Whether you think you can, or you think you can't - you're right."

11. Decision Making: We discovered strategies for making tough choices with confidence. Jeff Bezos' "regret minimization framework" is a powerful tool for making decisions aligned with your long-term vision.

12. Leadership Skills: We explored what it takes to be an effective leader in your business and life. Remember, leadership isn't about being in charge - it's about taking care of those in your charge.

13. The Power of Focus: We learned how to avoid distractions and stay laser-focused on what matters most. As Warren Buffett says, "The difference between successful people and really successful people is that really successful people say no to almost everything."

14. Work-Life Balance: We discovered the importance of taking care of yourself while building your business. Remember, you can't pour from an empty cup. Sustainable success: regular breaks, family time, and self-care—treating your wellbeing as a crucial business investment rather than an optional luxury.

15. Embracing Change: We explored how to adapt and thrive in an ever-changing business landscape. As Charles Darwin noted, it's not the strongest or the most intelligent who survive, but those most adaptable to change.

16. The Art of Delegation: We learned how to empower others and free up your time for high-level tasks. As an entrepreneur you do not work in the business but on the business. Remember Richard Branson's advice: "If you really want to grow as an entrepreneur, you've got to learn to delegate."

17. Emotional Intelligence: We discovered the power of understanding and managing emotions in business. Daniel Goleman's research shows that EQ is twice as important as IQ in predicting success. Throughout my career, I've watched emotionally intelligent leaders excel by reading situations accurately, handling conflicts gracefully, and building lasting relationships - skills that often matter more than raw intelligence.

18. The Power of Persistence: We explored what it takes to never give up on your dreams. Remember Thomas Edison's famous quote: "I have not failed. I've just found 10,000 ways that won't work." True persistence isn't stubbornness; it's the ability to adapt and keep moving forward. The most successful entrepreneurs I've known

weren't the most talented, but they were the ones who refused to stay down.

19. The Ethics Advantage: We learned how building a business with integrity can be your greatest competitive edge. As Warren Buffett says, "It takes 20 years to build a reputation and five minutes to ruin it."

Now, here's where the rubber meets the road. Knowledge is power, but only when it's applied. So how do you take all of this and turn it into real-world success? Here's your roadmap:

1. Start with Your Why: Simon Sinek's golden circle concept teaches us to start with why we do what we do. What's your purpose? What gets you out of bed in the morning? Define this, and you'll have a north star to guide all your decisions.

2. Set Clear, Compelling Goals: Break your vision down into specific, measurable goals. What do you want to achieve in the next year? The next 90 days? The next month? The next week? Share them with the team, friends and partners. Make these goals SMART: Specific, Measurable, Achievable, Relevant, and Time-bound.

3. Develop Your Growth Plan: Identify the skills and knowledge you need to achieve your goals. Create a learning plan to acquire these skills. No plan is a plan to fail. Remember, in the words of Eric Hoffer, "In times of change, learners inherit the earth, while the learned find themselves beautifully equipped to deal with a world that no longer exists."

4. Build Your Support Network: Surround yourself with people who believe in you and your vision. Find mentors, join mastermind groups, attend networking events and even virtual events online. Proximity is power. As Jim Rohn famously said, "You are the average of the five people you spend the most time with."

Chapter 20: Your Entrepreneurial Odyssey - Putting It All Together

5. Take Massive Action: Knowledge without action is useless. Start taking steps towards your goals every single day, no matter how small. The smallest action outweighs the noblest intention. Remember, it's not about taking the right first step - it's about taking a first step, then course-correcting as you go.

6. Embrace Failure and Learn: Remember, failure is not the opposite of success; it's part of success. Failures are like footprints on the path to mastery - each one shows you've dared to move forward. When things don't go as planned, ask yourself: "What can I learn from this? How can I use this to grow and take advantage?"

7. Practice Resilience: Develop strategies for bouncing back from setbacks. Resilience isn't about avoiding the storm - it's about building an umbrella of habits that keep you moving forward when it rains. This could include mindfulness practices, exercise, or simply having a strong support system to lean on during tough times.

8. Stay Focused: In a world full of distractions, your ability to focus on what truly matters is your superpower. Focus isn't about doing more things - it's about doing the right things longer. Use techniques like time-blocking and the Pomodoro method to maintain laser focus on your priorities.

9. Innovate Constantly: Set aside time regularly to brainstorm new ideas. How can you do things differently? How can you bring more value to your customers? The best innovations don't ask 'What's next?' but rather 'What's missing? Remember, innovation is not just about creating new products - it's about finding better ways to solve problems.

10. Lead with Emotional Intelligence: Develop your ability to understand and manage your own emotions and those of others. This will make you a more effective leader and help

you build stronger relationships in business and life. Great leaders read hearts as carefully as they read balance sheets.

11. Maintain Integrity: Build your business on a foundation of strong ethics. Remember, your reputation is your most valuable asset. Guard it fiercely. Your ethics are your signature - make sure every deal bears one that you're proud of.

12. Never Stop Learning: The entrepreneurial journey is one of constant growth. Commit to being a lifelong learner and always learning. Read books, attend workshops, attend networking events, seek out new experiences. As Socrates said, "The only true wisdom is in knowing you know nothing.

Now, I know what some of you are thinking. "Kay Kay, this sounds great, but it's overwhelming. Where do I even start?" And that's a fair question. The key is to start small, take tiny steps and build momentum.

So, here's your challenge: For the next 90 days, commit to taking one small action each day towards your entrepreneurial goals and document it. It could be as simple as reading an article about your industry, making one new networking connection, or spending 15 minutes brainstorming new ideas.

Will it be comfortable? Not always. Will there be days when you want to give up? Absolutely. But remember why you started this journey. Remember the impact you want to make, the life you want to create. The legacy you to leave for your family and others.

You have the power to turn your entrepreneurial dreams into reality. You can create a business and a life you love. And now, you have the mindset and the roadmap to make it happen.

So, are you ready? Are you ready to step into your power as an entrepreneur? Are you ready to start your journey towards the success you deserve? The choice is yours. And I believe in you.

Chapter 20: Your Entrepreneurial Odyssey - Putting It All Together

Entrepreneurship is a Marathon not a sprint. Let's transform your entrepreneurial vision into reality - methodically, strategically, relentlessly. Your future awaits not in dreams, but in daily purposeful action. The time for building your legacy isn't tomorrow, it's now. Make it happen.

Remember, being an entrepreneur is not just about what you do - it's about who you become in the process. It's about growing, learning, and constantly pushing yourself to new heights. As you embark on this journey, there will be ups and downs. There will be moments of exhilaration and moments of doubt. But here's the secret sauce: each of these experiences is shaping you into the successful entrepreneur you're meant to be every day.

Your journey matters. Your dreams matter. And when you show up every day, ready to give it your all, you give your ideas and your business the best chance to make the impact you're truly capable of.

So go forth with purpose, my fellow entrepreneur. Embrace the mindset. Take massive action. The success and fulfillment you dream of are waiting for you - all you need to do is start your journey and keep moving forward.

You've got this. Now go show the world what a determined, passionate entrepreneur can achieve. Your journey starts now. Make it count.

Action Steps:

1. Create Your 90-Day Action Plan: Based on the principles we've covered, set 3-5 key goals for the next 90 days. Break these down into daily actions.
2. Start a 'Mindset Journal': Each day, write down one limiting belief you're challenging and one empowering belief you're reinforcing.
3. Conduct a Skill Audit: Identify the top 3 skills you need to develop to achieve your goals. Create a learning plan for each.
4. Build Your Support Network: Reach out to 3 people who could support your entrepreneurial journey - a potential mentor, a peer, and someone you could mentor.
5. Schedule Your 'Big 3': Each day, identify the 3 most important tasks that will move you closer to your goals. Do these before anything else.

Key Takeaways:

- Success in entrepreneurship comes from consistently applying key principles and developing the right mindset.
- Your entrepreneurial journey is about personal growth as much as business growth.
- Taking consistent, aligned action is key to turning your entrepreneurial dreams into reality.
- Embracing failure, practicing resilience, and never stopping learning are crucial for long-term success.
- Your unique vision and values are your greatest assets - stay true to them throughout your journey.

Remember, your entrepreneurial journey is uniquely yours. Use these principles as a guide, but always trust your instincts and stay true to your vision. The world is waiting for the value only you can create. Now go forth and make your entrepreneurial dreams a reality!

Chapter 20: Your Entrepreneurial Odyssey - Putting It All Together

TAKE THE ENTREPRENEURIAL MINDSET ASSESSMENT AGAIN:

Rate yourself on a scale of 1-5 for each statement below:
1 = Strongly Disagree
2 = Disagree
3 = Neutral
4 = Agree
5 = Strongly Agree

1. I see failures as learning opportunities rather than personal defects. Rating: ___

2. I actively seek out challenges that push me out of my comfort zone. Rating: ___

3. I'm comfortable taking calculated risks in pursuit of my goals. Rating: ___

4. When faced with obstacles, I persist and find alternative solutions. Rating: ___

5. I regularly set ambitious goals for myself and work diligently to achieve them. Rating: ___

6. I'm open to feedback and criticism, seeing them as chances to improve. Rating: ___

7. I believe my skills and abilities can be developed through effort and learning. Rating: ____

8. I'm quick to adapt my strategies when circumstances change. Rating: ____

9. I actively look for opportunities where others see problems. Rating: ____

10. I take full responsibility for my successes and failures. Rating: ____

11. I regularly step out of my comfort zone to learn new skills. Rating: ____

12. I'm comfortable with uncertainty and ambiguity in business situations. Rating: ____

13. I network actively and build relationships with diverse groups of people. Rating: ____

14. I consistently follow through on my commitments, even when it's difficult. Rating: ____

15. I'm able to maintain a positive outlook, even in challenging situations. Rating: ____

Scoring:
Add up your total score: _____

60-75: Strong Entrepreneurial Mindset
45-59: Developing Entrepreneurial Mindset
30-44: Emerging Entrepreneurial Mindset
15-29: Beginning Entrepreneurial Mindset

Reflection:

1. Which areas did you score highest now?

Chapter 20: Your Entrepreneurial Odyssey - Putting It All Together

2. Which areas do you feel still needs the most improvement?

3. What specific actions can you take to strengthen your entrepreneurial mindset now?

> "This assessment serves as a foundation for your journey ahead. As you apply the tips and techniques explored throughout this book, you'll develop a robust toolkit of strategies to enhance all aspects of your life. Remember to revisit this assessment periodically; it's not just a measure of where you've been, but a compass pointing toward your future growth. Each time you return to it, you'll find new insights and opportunities for progress. Your journey of self-improvement is ongoing, and with each step, you're creating a more fulfilled and capable version of yourself. Embrace the path ahead, for your greatest achievements are yet to come."

Your Entrepreneurial Growth Begins Now!!!!!

Notes

1. Carol Dweck's research on growth and fixed mindsets: https://www.nature.com/articles/s41586-019-1466-y
2. Study on students transitioning to junior high school: https://bingschool.stanford.edu/news/carol-dweck-praising-intelligence-costs-childrens-self-esteem-and-motivation
3. Journal of Entrepreneurship study on growth mindset and entrepreneurial success: https://www.stratfordjournal.org/journals/index.php/journal-of-entrepreneurship-proj/article/download/1720/2232/5441
4. Sara Blakely and the founding of Spanx: https://www.fundable.com/learn/startup-stories/spanx
5. Elon Musk and SpaceX: https://www.space.com/25355-elon-musk-60-minutes-interview.html
6. James Dyson's vacuum cleaner development: https://www.dyson.com/james-dyson
7. Roger Bannister breaking the four-minute mile in 1954: https://en.wikipedia.org/wiki/Roger_Bannister
8. Airbnb's transformation of the travel industry: https://www.cascade.app/studies/dyson-strategy-study
9. Brené Brown's research on vulnerability and innovation: https://www.psychologicalscience.org/observer/dweck-growth-mindsets
10. Percy Spencer's accidental invention of the microwave oven: https://blogs.loc.gov/inside_adams/2021/01/microwaves/
11. The invention of Post-It Notes: https://www.invent.org/blog/trends-stem/who-invented-post-it-notes
12. Stanford University's Neuroscience Institute research: https://www.psychologicalscience.org/observer/dweck-growth-mindsets
13. Journal of Business Venturing study: https://www.tandfonline.com/doi/full/10.1080/23311975.2024.2314733

14. [Mark Zuckerberg's quote on risk-taking:
    https://online.hbs.edu/blog/post/growth-mindset-vs-fixed-mindset](https://online.hbs.edu/blog/post/growth-mindset-vs-fixed-mindset)
15. [Thomas Edison's light bulb invention:](#)
16. https://www.archives.gov/milestone-documents/thomas-edisons-patent-application-for-the-light-bulb

www.ingramcontent.com/pod-product-compliance
Lightning Source LLC
Chambersburg PA
CBHW052147220526
45471CB00004B/1561